W9-BZB-575

WHERE DO GRANDMOTHERS COME FROM?
(And where do they go?)

Also by Frances Weaver

MIDLIFE MUSINGS
SPEAKING OF THE GIRLS
THE GIRLS WITH THE GRANDMOTHER FACES
AS FAR AS I CAN SEE . . .
THIS YEAR I PLAN TO GO ELSEWHERE
GOLDEN ROAMERS (A NOVEL)

On audio tape
THE GIRLS WITH THE GRANDMOTHER FACES

Frances Weaver's books are available at
special bulk-purchase discounts for sales promotions,
premiums, or fund-raisings. Special books or book excerpts
can be created to fit specific needs.
For details, write
Midlife Musings, Publisher,
P. O. Box 970, Saratoga Springs, New York 12866,
or call (800) 842-7229.

WHERE DO GRANDMOTHERS COME FROM?
(And where do they go?)

A close look at four generations, in three parts

FRANCES WEAVER

With incidental drawings
from the author's sketchbook

MIDLIFE MUSINGS

Saratoga Springs
New York
1992

Copyright © 1992 by Frances Weaver

All rights reserved.
No part of this publication may be reproduced, stored in a retrieval system, or
transmitted, in any form or by any means, electronic, mechanical, photocopying,
recording, or otherwise, without the prior written permission of the Publisher,
except that reviewers may quote short passages
provided they include proper credit.

ISBN 0-9617930-4-X

Cover design:
Melanie Wegner
Alstrom / Peña Creative Services
Albuquerque, New Mexico

Book design, editing and production:
Wallace W. Abbey
Piñon Consulting
Pueblo, Colorado

Printed in the United States of America

10 9 8 7 6 5 4 3 2

Published by
Midlife Musings
P. O. Box 970
Saratoga Springs, New York 12866

CONTENTS

FOREWORD

I first knew Frances Weaver as a renowned newspaper columnist, television commentator, after-dinner speaker, and widow of a past president of the Rotary Club of Pueblo, and then as the nice lady I once met in a filling station who seemed uncertain about where to put the gasoline into her Bavarian sedan.

Then one day I got a call from a frantic Frances. Could I help her outwit her new laptop computer? Well, one thing led professionally to another, and here we are. Now I also know what thousands of senior citizens knew long ago: that Frances Allison Weaver also writes books. And also publishes books.

And also is dedicated to convincing the world's other grandmothers that life is still fun even when it's seen through wrinkled eyes.

Is the story she tells in these pages real? Oh, yes! If your age is, well, uh, *advanced*, I'll second Frances's notion that this could be your story, too. I can tell you that if you'd change McPherson to Cherryvale and Hubbell's to Squier Drug it would pretty much be mine.

Read this book, please.

There are messages here for us grandparents, and memories.

Wally Abbey
Pueblo, Colorado

PROLOGUE

Most of our lives, we ask questions. From the first days of being able to talk at all, we have asked, "why?" and "how?" and "where?" Every child has sooner or later asked, "where do babies come from?" and most of them have received some pretty silly answers.

Now, from the other end of the lifeline spectrum, I find myself asking my own version of a similar question. Observing the reactions of my family and friends to grandmotherhood, I'm wondering: "where did some of these grandmothers come from?"

The children of the world certainly have an assortment of grandmothers! Some prefer to be called anything but Grandmother, using instead some Shirley Temple name like DeeDee or Mimsie. Other women seem to have been born to be grandmothers. Their entire being—their days, nights, and weekends—center on those second-generation offspring. Some of us hope we live between these two extremes.

We have all "come from" the same source: our own childhood and earlier adult life. Our education, family loyalty, ethical structure, and general outlook on life took shape during the 40 or 50 years before we found ourselves faced with the role played in our own lives by women of two generations ago. How we behave in that role, how much we enjoy or make the most of this phase of family life, depends on what sort of "baggage" we bring along.

Knowing full well I cannot speak for more than one woman, I choose on these pages to explore my own heritage, childhood, and parenting years in an effort to explain where *this* grandmother came from. Along the way, many of my peer group will certainly see reflections of themselves.

That's what books like this are all about.

♣

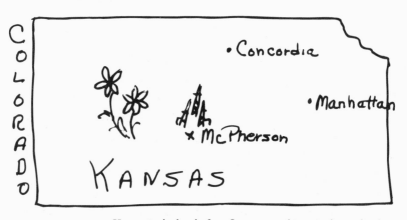

Kansas is the land of sunflowers, sunshine, and sonsabitches.
—*Joe Weaver*
Concordia, Kansas

I

SUNFLOWERS, SUNSHINE, AND SONSABITCHES

It all started in Kansas.

Oh, Mother's father had come to McPherson from his native Denmark before the turn of the century. He and his three brothers immigrated to establish life for themselves in the new world instead of being conscripted into the Kaiser's army when Germany took over their section of Denmark. After experimenting with their new land in parts of Iowa and Oregon, for reasons long lost to the rest of us, the Jensen brothers chose to settle in Kansas in the butter-and-egg business at which so many Danes excel.

Dad's family on his father's side had been working its way more slowly westward, having put out from England for Jamestown Colony in 1609 or shortly thereafter.

Both of our grandmothers seemed to have sprung from well-mixed American stock, so we could fit in genealogically almost anywhere.

Most of the people in McPherson had the same sort of heritage. Some of the Swedes were first generation, but it had not taken the Lindstroms and the Petersons long to mix in with the Schmidts and the Fergusons. Of the five thousand population, more or less, most of us fit this one pattern—no wide cultural mix here. McPherson folks were Lutherans, Methodists, Baptists, and Presbyterians. The Germans on the farms around town were Mennonites. A family of Episcopalians moved into town, we heard, but they soon became Methodists. The Jewish family living on our block were our friends like everyone else in town. Their differences were not crucial to McPherson social circles. Two black couples living among us were treated as equals, certainly, but they had to go over to Hutchinson to go swimming.

Both of my parents were born in and grew up in McPherson. We were a very stable community. The railroad came through several times a day, passenger and freight. Our roads led to more exciting places—Salina or Wichita. Our farmers had big barns and amber waves of grain that would have warmed the heart of Katherine Lee Bates even if we lacked the purple mountains' majesty by about 300 miles.

Down by the railroad station was the deer park, which had been there since my parents had been kids. Everyone went by to see the deer in the park—a full city block with plenty of good grass and all of McPherson to make sure the deer thrived there.

Three or four blocks away we had Memorial Park. Right behind the courthouse. That courthouse still stands there, wonderful gray stone with a fine tower with a clock. On the walls of that venerable building hang pictures of our Grandfather Allison from his days as mayor before I was even born in 1924. Uncle George Allison's "judge" pictures hang there, too.

On the corner of the courthouse block, just across from the Elks Club, stood the jail. For some reason, that always seemed like a joke to my elders— the jail and the Elks so close together. North of the jail there remained a horse trough from horse and buggy days, right beside a table where old men played dominoes under the trees. Believe me, this could have been the set for *Our Town* and most of us would have fit into the story.

McPherson had been named for General James Birdseye McPherson. From the Civil War, we had been told. A statue of that dignified gentleman astride his horse stands at the west entrance to the courthouse, to be admired from and surrounded by the beauty of the park. Every town ought to have its own statue of a hero or some sort of a memorial, and General McPherson stands unchallenged right there between the courthouse and the flower beds, guarding and preserving McPherson for all of us.

Childhood memories never really disappear entirely, do they? Someone said to me not too long ago, "Every day you have to decide, am I gonna' be the statue or the bird?" and immediately I saw General McPherson there in the park, and shuddered to think of the birds.

Some civic-minded benefactor of McPherson had seen to it that every known variety of tree grew in that park behind the courthouse. When we had nature study in Girl Scouts, our leaf scrapbooks would have been the envy of Scouts all over central Kansas. We even had gingko trees in that park. Fully half of the people I know today, my age, have no idea about a gingko tree, unless they have seen them in Japan or the cities of the East—but not in Kansas, for heaven's sake.

Swimming and floating under the vast variety of shade and ornamental trees of our park were a collection of the biggest goldfish west of any given point. Maybe the tree enthusiast had also introduced the goldfish in the lily ponds. At any rate, it had to have been someone with very big ideas about what a town should have in the way of fish in ponds in parks.

Those suckers measured nearly two feet long, I'm sure. Calling them suckers does not demean the species. Those gold and white and orange and spotted babies were plain old carp, of course. But we loved watching them and made sure our cousins admired our goldfish whenever they came to town.

All sorts of civic festivities took place in the park, at least until we

had a bigger park on the east side of town, but that came later. One summer my dad served on the committee for a big picnic in the park— might have been Rotary, or the Young Republicans or some such. Anyway, Dad was charged with providing lemonade for the crowd, long before the days of frozen juices or dry drink mixes. Ever the resourceful fellow, good old Dad hooked up a brand new Maytag washer with numerous extension cords into the courthouse. There under General McPherson's watchful eye, my father made lemonade, running the lemons through that wringer to squeeze them, mixing them with water and sugar with the dasher going in the machine, and serving fine fresh lemonade through the hose meant to empty the machine.

My father, John Allison, progressed in the world of banking, oil and natural gas, and politics in the years to follow, but he will be forever remembered for that great lemonade.

McPherson teems with such memories at every turn.

Just telling that story brings back memories of washing machines and my father. Years later he was still convinced a Maytag was good for more than laundry, and claimed he could shell peas through the wringer of another, much older, machine. That made even more of a mess than the lemonade.

Not many tourists or visitors came to McPherson in those days of the thirties when I was growing up. Not many get there yet, I'd

assume. But did we ever have the crowds on May Day! That celebration—we called it "All Schools Day"—really brought spectators from as far away as Lindsborg and Galva and Canton, even some from as far as Newton. Thirty miles. Every school-age child in McPherson took part in that parade. The kindergarten youngsters had to ride in the back of a truck but the rest of us walked—no, marched—the entire four or five blocks of Main Street carrying helium-filled balloons of our school colors. We wore white, generally, and hated the May Days when our mothers decided we'd need sweaters. That messed up the color scheme.

Roosevelt School's colors were green and white. Lincoln students had red and white. Park School, purple and white. Then the new Washington School got blue and orange so none of their kids had to carry the dumb old white balloons. I hated them for that. But we marched, followed by bands and floats and people on tractors and horses. Everyone had some sort of a banner.

One bad thing about May Day happened when the folks from the country came to town and brought their picnic lunches. They sat on the manicured lawns of the "city folks" to eat chicken and dump lemonade all over. Every time I had to read the story about the city mouse and the country mouse I thought about May Day and those farmers with their potato salad.

No matter how unimpressive our surroundings might be, we can always find someone to ridicule and look down on, can't we?

May Day also meant the carnival set up on the street between the library and the courthouse. The Ferris wheel and the Octopus delighted most of us, but one unfortunate incident comes up in talking about that carnival. That near-tragedy occurred when some woman riding the Ferris wheel became very sick and threw up just as her seat reached the top of the wheel, splattering the crowd below and ruining Miss Rankin's flowered hat. Miss Rankin taught home ec. We assumed the sick lady must have come from some smaller town, like Galva or Windom.

The parade and all of the celebration always took over the town on the first Wednesday in May. Think how old-fashioned that is: Our biggest annual holiday had nothing to do with a three-day weekend. Maybe it does now. I hope not. We lost enough of the May Day feeling when we no longer gave May baskets to our friends.

Remember May baskets? Almost everyone I talk to seems to have known about May baskets. Everyone in their 60s, anyway. We made baskets of construction paper of various colors. Most we fashioned like a funnel fastened with paste on one side, but some show-off girls made theirs of fancy folds and attached a handle. These beauties we filled with lilacs, tulips, and/or iris (peonies wouldn't bloom until the end of May, in time for Decoration Day), then we added a candy treat or two.

Down the street we'd go, sort of a reverse trick-or-treat night. The trick was to hang your basket on the doorknob, ring the doorbell and run like blazes. We hoped our special friend would answer the door to find the basket. The treat came when your intended receiver stepped out on the porch, looking up and down the block to find out who had left such a gift. We hid in the bushes, of course, and giggled.

What happened to May baskets? On our newsreel screens we saw Russians celebrating what they claimed to be their special holiday, May Day, and everyone stopped with the baskets. Just as during World War I no red-blooded American would be found acting like a German, so in the late '30s none of us dared to risk being called Communists because we celebrated May Day. How easily we have given up some of our best traditions.

☙

Even in all-WASP McPherson we had ethnic humor. The butt of all the jokes were the Swedes. For some reason, those good people had the reputation of being slower than the rest of us, so we heard cracks like, "The next thing dumber than a dumb Irishman is a good smart Swede."

My own Danish grandfather regaled us with his poem about ten thousand Swedes who ran through the weeds chased by one sick Norwegian. We laughed and carried on jokingly about the Swedish people in our town and in nearby Lindsborg, but when Christmastime came, we were more than ready to join in enjoying their feasts of fancy breads and their lingonberries. Today the Swedish heritage of the area, especially Lindsborg, charms us all with little red wooden horses and ornaments made of straw.

I might be the only one left who remembers the dumb Irishman joke, and I've only been in McPherson twice in the past 20 years.

☙

To understand and visualize this tree-filled, mid-America personified, we might as well start at Hubbell's. Generally speaking, everything in town started with Hubbell's.

Business men stopped at Hubbell's Drug Store on the way from the post office first thing in the morning; and that put McPherson into gear for the day. Right there on Main Street, across from the Helstrom Theatre, the *McPherson Daily Republican,* and the McPherson & Citizens Bank, on the same block with Upshaw's Furniture, Houghton's Bakery and Sweeney's Shoe Store, Hubbell's was the hub, no doubt about that. Anything worth hearing or seeing was seen or heard at Hubbell's. From the pressed-tin ceiling to the white tiny-tile floor, Hubbell's represented our town—our version of mid-America during the New Deal.

The soda jerks at Hubbell's made those delectable ice cream sodas with the weird sort of foam the bubbles of which popped into a sort of scum that left the glass looking even worse than buttermilk did. They dispensed cherry phosphates and lemon Cokes and fresh limeade. All day long, half of McPherson occupied those stools at the counter or the spindly chairs at the wire-legged tables, in shifts. You knew who'd be in Hubbell's by what time it was. Events of the day were discussed and observed while prescriptions were filled and purchases of cold cream, witch hazel, cascara, hot water bottles, Epsom salts and psyllium seed kept Louie busy behind his counters.

Very nearly every woman in town passed through Hubbell's on the way to the balcony to Reva's to get her hair done. Reva's Vogue Beauty Salon featured marcels, boyish bobs, and permanent waves that involved use of a machine almost guaranteed to turn out customers smelling like a singed chicken.

The women under the dryers sat peering over the balcony at the drug store customers. Once in a while, one would comment or pass on the latest gossip in a voice loud enough to be heard in the next county, forgetting she was out-shouting the dryer.

My sisters and I, still in grade school, had our hair done by Reva or her assistant. In the days before detergent shampoos, just getting the soap out of a little girl's hair, or keeping it out of her eyes, made hair-washing a chore. Mother must have sent all of us to Reva for no more tears.

You of the same generation and basic background as the Hubbell's crowd might be wondering by now if Hubbell's had curb service.

Natural question. Of course they did.

One of the great treats of a summer afternoon or evening was to find a parking space in front of Hubbell's so Frank Zimmermen or one of the other cute car-hops could bring cones and cokes on a tray made to hook over the door of a Hudson or a Studebaker with the window open. Conversation went on between cars with everyone checking to see who was there with who else.

A&W cut into the curb-service business when they moved in a block down the street with the first real drive-in, offering free little tiny mugs of root beer for kids under five. There was a miniature golf course down that direction, too. But we can assume the faithful remained at Hubbell's.

If any town can be described in one word, the word for McPherson is *flat*.

McPherson was so flat the only way to use a sled was to pull it, often behind a car. Dangerous as that sounds, we did it regularly, since no street in the whole town had enough of a grade to sled down on our own. Snow we had. Hills we lacked. But we still insisted on sleds.

Neither was McPherson the best town in the world for swimming, in the earliest days of our youth. The only pool in town open to the public belonged to the Sundahls. To me, trying to learn to put my head under water or dog paddle all the way across, Sundahl's Pool seemed enormous.

The water temperature varied daily, depending on the day of the week. Sundahl operated on a strictly drain-and-fill routine: fill on Saturday, drain the next Friday. Mr Sundahl had no worries with filters or water treatment or heaters. By Thursday the pool temperature reached dishwater ranges and the bottom took on a greenish cast where you could see it at all. Some of us slipped a lot on that mossy bottom near the end of the week, but by noon on Saturday the moss had been swept and hosed away and crystal-clear water again filled our swimming pool. Of course, anyone daring to plunge into Sundahl's on Saturday immediately turned blue.

The water drained from Sundahl's Pool (by Friday well fortified with nitrogen from the kiddie pool, I'm sure) ran straight down a ditch into Mr. Madden's truck garden. Mr. Madden's tomatoes and cucumbers and watermelon, as well as his unbeatable sweet corn, loved Sundahl's as much as we did.

"Compact" might fit our town, too. Directly across from the court-house with the park and the trees and the goldfish stood the library. Behind the library, the band stand. On Wednesday nights in summer, the center of town moved just one block north when the entire population turned out to hear the concerts by our prize-winning band. It could play anything. There would be lightning bugs around, older folks sat in their cars or on benches, we played tag and ate

popcorn and listened to the band. The big kids picked on the littler ones, and horns on the cars honked rousing applause at the end of every number.

During those terrible summers of the drought the band concerts lost a bit of appeal because of the swarms of grasshoppers around, even after dark. It's a wonder the grasshoppers didn't clog up the cornets. Maybe they did. At any rate, those Dust Bowl days made a lasting impression, band concerts and all.

We four girls and our neighbors walked only one block to Roosevelt School. On the days of the dust storms, about my third and fourth grades, we had to wait at the school for a grown-up to take us home. Small children could suffocate or get lost in the thick dust and die out there.

Like a hurricane or a tornado, a dust storm cannot be believed until you've been through one. We would see the dark cloud rolling in, slowly, with almost no sound. We could feel the dust between our teeth, could watch it settle on our desks and on our clothes, even though the windows were closed. Intense heat and lack of rain had left the trees bare, stripped by the grasshoppers who found no grass or bugs left for their normal diet. Eventually, the grasshoppers ate the clothes off the lines and the curtains out of the windows. Really!

Those Mormons with their infestations of locusts have always had my sympathy. When a swarm of hungry insects takes over your world,

it's like outer space. Science fiction. Alfred Hitchcock missed the boat by not making a movie of McPherson in those days. We were a sight.

McPherson could have been called a sight for sore eyes during the Great Depression. While the rest of the world opened soup kitchens and took jobs with the WPA, some clever soul discovered several oil fields in our part of Kansas and we were off and running.

Those days, our family lived in a small house on south Maple Street, down near the Free Methodist College and close to Roosevelt School. Ann turned ten in 1933. The rest of us were younger, but we all recall vividly our dad coming in smelling of oil. His good hat was spattered, his boots tracked oily mud through our newly-remodeled house. We moved to a bigger house.

Our town not only survived the depression, it and we flourished in the oil business. About that time a small refinery was built beyond the south end of town and McPherson has smelled like oil ever since. Once you get used to it, the small of oil becomes less offensive. It becomes more like the smell of money.

The towers of the refinery on the south end of town balanced in a very real way the towering grain elevators of the Wall-Rogalsky Milling Company in the north end. Those architectural geniuses claiming to have invented the idea of "form and function" (Bauhaus?) must have been inspired by grain elevators. Except perhaps for a lighthouse, no structure is more compelling to my eye than a grain elevator rising out of the prairie—pure, proud, essential to the world around it, whether lined up by the hundreds in Chicago or Kansas City or standing sentry-duty on the western Kansas plains, two, four, six at a time. I honestly appreciate the clean, gleaming cylindrical elevators just as a native New Yorker adores the Chrysler Building or an Athenian venerates the Parthenon.

We took it all for granted, the mill and the refinery.
Our town stood firmly on the land, the grain, and the oil.

❧

2
WHO LIVES IN A TOWN LIKE THAT?

Strange as it seems, I talk about and write about my childhood years in Kansas as if our small town has disappeared, like I'm writing about Rosita, Colorado, or some other ghost town. Not true, of course, but those of us who were born and raised before World War II do consider that time and place (whatever place) downright ghostly when we contemplate the changes in our society and in our world.

Going back to McPherson today the city limits have not moved much; the general topography hasn't changed. Anyone will still say, "this is a nice little town," but it's not the same town. Just as Pueblo, Colorado, bears little resemblance for those who grew up here when they return; just as any other "home town" affects its native sons and daughters, these past five decades have changed our towns, and our lives.

Therefore, if I seem to be referring to a "town that used to be," in a sense that's true. My McPherson fits into the same frame on the map. The time frame doesn't fit any more.

Jacks and jump ropes, games of kick the can and punch the icebox, home-made ice cream and Harvey Houses, quarantine signs and Bank Night at the show, hired girls and Helen Trent—all are buzz words from any pre-television growing-up. (Hired girl: That was a good strong German girl from the farm who hired out for five dollars a week and room and board to wait out her days until she was claimed in marriage and could chase children of her own.)

The town whistle started every day for us. At seven o'clock the whistle sounded at the power plant over by the railroad yards. They blew it again at noon and at six o'clock. We all set our watches and our days by the whistle. Somehow I recall a later blast—like nine o'clock at night—but I'm not certain. Maybe I just made that up. At any rate, we knew when to get up and when to eat lunch and dinner every day without fail.

School started at nine for grade school. At good old Roosevelt, Mr. Smith, the good old janitor, strode up and down between the two front doors hand-ringing the school bell. We lined up instantly. Five minutes later he rang the tardy bell. By that time we were all in our places ready for the beginning "morning exercises:" the salute to the flag, maybe a song, and health habits.

Our teacher asked the same questions every morning:

"Did you brush your teeth before coming to school?"

"Did you drink eight glasses of water yesterday?"

"Did you get eight hours sleep?"

"Do you have a clean handkerchief?"

These days, I wonder if anyone asks any kid at school if he has brushed his teeth, but that was big business in my day.

The same emphasis on routine bound our days together. We wrote the spelling words 20 times or more, we recited times tables and wrote them over and over again, too. I majored in push-pulls and ovals for the penmanship classes. Those lines and lines of even ovals written with a "dip" pen and the push-pulls all with the same slant on the page really made my day.

I still love handwriting. Art, music, gym, Bible, were afternoon special classes, but school and recess basically come back to me as pleasant times.

I'll take that back. School I liked. Recess was hell when we jumped rope, because none of the girls in my grade ever got a turn after Sadie Ann Gallee started to jump.

She never missed, so we'd stand on one foot or the other all lined up for another turn to jump the rope when the girl ahead of us would trip or stumble on the rope. Sadie Ann never gave us a chance. Her damnable curls kept bouncing and she kept right on jumping even when the girls turning the rope gave her "high waters." Just miserable. She jumped her way through "Grace, Grace, dressed in lace," "Ella,

Ella, kissed her fella," and "Teddy bear, teddy bear, go upstairs," while the rest of us secretly wished she'd hang herself on the rope. Before we knew it, Mr. Smith was ringing the bell again and we had to go back in.

Playing jacks occupied more of our time than any other activity, I think. We had piano lessons to practice and such, but every free moment was spent sitting on the sidewalk with one or two friends, going through the games of jacks. My fingernails on my right hand can still feel that way—when the nails were completely worn down on the "outside" from scooping up the jacks from the concrete.

We played other games, too, outdoors. In our neighborhood we were four girls; across the street lived four Lawson girls; the O'Briens down the block had so many kids I lost count—but they sure made for a good game of hide-and-seek.

Other youngsters drifted in and out of our orbit on Maple Street, like Charlotte Hornbeck, who lived next door for a while, but I never did get along with her. She always wanted something I wanted, I guess.

Late afternoon my sisters and I gathered to watch the radio. We sat in front of the Majestic in time for *Little Orphan Annie* and *Jack Armstrong, the All-American Boy*. We sang along:

"Who's the little chatterbox, the one with pretty auburn locks?" We really hit it on "*arff* goes Sandy."

The radio gained importance as we grew. By the time we were in junior high and high school, we raced home for lunch every day to catch the latest crises in the lives of *Ma Perkins* and *Our Gal Sunday*. Fifteen minutes at a crack. Those people endured such personal tragedy as the suspected theft of an engagement ring from *Mary Noble, Backstage Wife*, to another unsuccessful attempt of Helen Trent to snag a man (usually the elusive Gil) after 35.

Evening radio entertained the entire family. On Sunday nights we loved to spend "this hour" with Eddie Cantor as much as he claimed loving spending it with us. We knew all of the folks who lived in Allen's Alley and laughed ourselves silly over Jack Benny and Mary Livingstone. Friday nights we heard *Grand Central Station* and *Lux Radio Theatre*. Barbara Luddy, Lester Tremaine—familiar names at our house; and, of course, Carlton E. Morse and the Barbour Family.

We listened to and delighted in the birth of singing commercials. Twelve full ounces of Pepsi-Cola for a nickel, Rinso White whistles, or jingles about Barbasol or Ovaltine. To us they were Burma Shave signs set to music. Remember Burma Shave?

SCHOOL AHEAD/PLEASE GO SLOW/

LET OUR LITTLE/SHAVERS GROW/

BURMA SHAVE

DON'T STICK YOUR ELBOW/OUT TOO FAR/

IT MIGHT GO HOME/IN ANOTHER CAR/

BURMA SHAVE

DON'T PASS CARS/ON CURVE OR HILL/

IF THE COPS DON'T GET YOU/

THE MORTICIANS WILL/

BURMA SHAVE

What else did our family do before television? We went for rides. I cannot imagine any of my children saying to their families, "Let's go for a ride."

John and I didn't do that very much with our children, either, but one of the joys of our lives came when we piled into the back seat, fighting to sit by the window, and spent an hour or so on a Sunday afternoon or a summer evening just riding around McPherson. We'd see friends in their yards and stop while the fathers swapped jokes and we played with their kids. Sometimes we'd drive out into the country. Usually our rides ended with a root beer or at the curb in front of Hubbell's.

At one point—I must have been at least four years old—Dad and some buddies bought an airplane. A Bellanca biplane, I think it was called. For a while on Sunday afternoons we would ride out to a pasture out north of town and look at the wondrous airplane.

Each Sunday Dad would insist that we would just love riding in that airplane.

Each Sunday I, for one, allowed as how I would wait until next Sunday.

To hear Daddy tell about it years later, I bragged for quite some time about how I would ride high in the sky next Sunday. Of course that Sunday never came. I still shudder over small planes.

We put in a lot of front-porch time, too. Time and again I have written about what I consider to be one of the causes of the breakup of American family life, the demise of the front porch. Along our street, particularly after we moved to Walnut Street where Grandmother lived across the street, the social life of the whole area took place on an absolutely open and friendly basis, one front porch to the next. When our cousins were visiting we'd drink lemonade and listen to the grown-ups on the porch for a while, then go out to play "mother, may I?" under the street lamp on the corner.

Grandmother Allison's bachelor brother, Uncle Bill, was always on the porch. He'd tell us stories we'd already heard, then give us grand gifts of the empty silver bottles in which he bought his "tonic." Nobody—but nobody—would have accused dear old Uncle Bill of having a drinking problem (he just napped a lot) but the labels on those silver tonic bottles listing the alcohol content did make one wonder.

And on the hot days when Uncle Bill could be found stretched out napping on the front lawn of the high school, his enormous bare feet attracting the attention of passing motorists, some of us worried a bit about the old boy. Kansas was "dry" in those days; tonics like Uncle Bill's must have been very popular. Forerunner to Geritol, I guess. Uncle Bill lived with Grandmother for a long time, I'd suppose. I cannot remember a time when he was not a part of the household.

Two of my grandparents died when I was barely old enough to have known them, my Grandfather Allison and my Grandmother Jensen. Both of the surviving grandparents had wonderful places for children to play, so a visit to either meant much in our young lives.

Grandmother Allison lived close to us for many years. Her home fascinated us because of the nooks and crannies. We never tired of being at Grandmother's. My dad and his six older sisters had grown up in that ample, rather clumsy Victorian house. The front porch turned the corner to be twice as big as expected, with a porch swing and newfangled "gliders" plus wicker chairs. The living room had two sections, too, plus a "middle room" or study, which must have been Grandfather's domain, with a huge desk we could hide under.

It must have been this house that gave me my penchant for porches. The sleeping porch spanned the back, with beds for at least eight people. That sleeping porch was the world's greatest place to tell ghost stories to frighten younger cousins. We'd wait until Grandmother was snoring peacefully in her bed at the end of the porch, then start in on the little kids. On hot nights or at nap time, we could count on Grandmother to hand out cornstarch bags. With heat rash, chigger bites and the rest of our itches, we adored Grandmother's cornstarch bags.

Almost as much as we would have loved makeup. We forever fussed over Grandmother with all sorts of potions, mostly witch hazel and Pond's cold cream. She had the patience of some sort of a saint. Her hair would be combed and brushed, then clumsily braided. We smeared her with rouge and Tangee lipstick samples.

More often than not, Grandmother Allison had handwork projects for us to tackle. We learned to crochet and to make patchwork quilts for our dolls. My handicrafts never met the standards of my sisters. Ann and Middy made cute little crocheted purses with bracelets for handles, but I never got past the chain-stitch stage. I had a chain of chain-stitch about 40 feet long, but it never became a purse with a bracelet handle.

Paper dolls were big business, lying on the floor in the middle room cutting figures from Sears catalogues. Finding a full-length girl complete with both feet took most of the afternoon. Then finding dresses to fit with the arms in the right positions became a major chore. Once in a while we settled for the *Tillie the Toiler* paper dolls in the funny papers, but the catalog ones lasted longer. Heavier paper.

Gram's bathroom upstairs had a tub with feet, of course, and the walls had been "done" by a local artisan who had used a turkey feather to make the white walls into fake marble. They tell me that's a lost art, and I'm not surprised.

The second bathroom was downstairs and had been originally what our grandfather invented as the "fuss room." Any child of the seven not behaving according to his standards spent time in the "fuss room" contemplating better patterns of behavior. Since my dad's oldest sister must have been at least 20 years older than he, that room saw many years of use.

That bathroom had two doors—to the dining room and to the "den." We had to be very careful to close both doors tightly, even when in a desperate hurry, or we could be heard using the toilet by everyone in the house. I know. That dread accident happened to me once when the preacher sat in the living room. My mother had a fit I have not forgotten yet.

The back stairs and the attic steps—and the basement, come to think of it—had secret places. The steps were in three short flights around these openings big enough to hide in. The attic held every marvel from the old Edison phonograph to trunks of clothes including Grandmother's wedding dress. We played our favorite record, *Where Did Robinson Crusoe Go With Friday on Saturday Night?* over and over again, singing along with Mr. Gallagher and Mr. Sheehan.

Years later, when our own children played those scratchy thick records on an Edison at their Weaver grandparents', I was just as tickled as I had been in my own childhood.

The basement had it all: a fruit cellar with jars of all sorts and conditions of preserves, jellies and pickles; a cellar door; a cistern where Gram collected rainwater to wash her long gray hair so her braids always shone in the sunlight.

We played in the basement mostly on Mondays, while Grandmother and Esther, her hired girl, were doing the laundry. We were allowed to help with the washing when rinse time came. We ran all that stuff through the wringer. Two tubs stood by the west wall near the outside steps to the back yard. Gram must have had a hose to fill the washer—didn't everybody?—and the smell of Fels Naptha filled the basement. Esther rejoiced when Rinso and other boxed granulated soaps replaced the bars that Gram preferred.

Our "job" involved straightening the towels and sheets and napkins as best we could because the wringer balked at big lumps of wet linens. After one load had been wrung through to the first tub, the wringer had to be swung around so we could wring the whole mess into the second rinse tub. No matter how I tried, I could never position that wringer so most of the "wrung-out" water didn't go on the floor. What a mess! The rinsed-out soap made the floor slippery.

Eventually, one load at a time (whites first, socks and rags last), the heavy baskets were toted up to the yard. It occurred to me at the time that Esther spent all day Monday with a mouth full of clothespins. Mountains of clean-smelling laundry piled on the dining room table made the whole day worth while. Grandmother and Esther stayed in her house, as did Grandmother's neighbor ladies because they had chores like laundry that filled one day at a time and reinforced their reason for being there.

While the clothes dried, we stayed in the back yard. There were swings in the trees and a chicken yard behind the garage. I wish I had painted that alley. Enormous elm and maple trees met over

Grandmother's alley to make a green tunnel. Back fences hid under Queen Anne's lace and masses of sweet peas. Bachelor buttons and orange poppies lined the roadway. That alley looked like a Lovers' Lane for Jeanette McDonald and Nelson Eddy. Hollyhocks bloomed higher than we could reach. Basic midwest.

My grandmother never drove a car and she stayed home a lot. She never yelled at us, either. And the ginger cookies at her house have never been equaled in my 66 years.

Grandmother's house attracted a lot of bums. The Rock Island yards on the west edge of town were less than four blocks from our houses, and some way the word got around over there about the good food at 220 South Walnut. Maybe arrows on the sidewalks led to Grandmother's latticed back porch. Often in those Depression days we'd hear a knock at that back door and we could peek through the lattice to see a dirty man in old clothes standing there asking for food. Grandmother or Esther would feed them there on the porch in spite of warnings from the rest of the family that they would be murdered in their beds some night by one of those hoboes. Grandmother never argued. She just went on feeding the tramps and smiling when they thanked her. Once in a while they'd get to do some chores around the house, but not often. Doing Grandmother's chores belonged to Charlie Rogers.

No way could I guess how many years Charlie Rogers had been handyman for my grandparents in McPherson. I do know Charlie must have been around the house about twice a week because something always needed fixing. Most of all, he fixed the kitchen door. That door led from the end of the kitchen to a smaller porch where Esther usually had pickles or home-made kraut aging in a crock. The door would sag at regular intervals, generally after a rain. Then it would stick.

Charlie, being summoned once more on account of the kitchen door, would remove the door from its hinges, lay it out on saw horses on the bigger part of the back porch, and perform his standard procedure: He sawed a wedge off the bottom of the door and tacked it onto the top. Same wedge. He then rehung the door, which no longer stuck. However, that door had a window, about a two-foot-square window, supposedly in the top half of the door. So many times had Charlie performed this operation, the window sat at about a 20-

degree angle, but "as long as a body could see through it" that surely didn't bother Grandmother or Esther.

I wonder now what might have happened if the door had begun sticking at the top instead of the bottom. Charlie could have straightened the window.

cs

Our maternal grandparents, the Jensens, had moved to Redlands, California, about the time Ann was born, so it was to Redlands that we trekked summer after summer to visit our Grandaddy Chris.

That man—Lord, we thought he was old—lived in the middle of a small orange grove. I suppose it could not have been more than five acres, but to us the rows of trees and irrigation ditches seemed endless.

We had girl cousins near our own age in California. As a matter of fact, we grew up pretty short of boy cousins.

In the center of Grandad's orange grove two trees had been cut out. This open secluded space became our special place. We convinced ourselves (my sisters, cousins and me) that our mothers had no idea where we might be. In that sanctuary we had our palm-leaf

factory. We made anything we found possible out of palm leaves, but if you've ever tried to cut through a palm frond you know how tough those fibers can be, and we were not allowed to take sharp knives from the kitchen. So most of our palm-leaf products turned out to be fans.

But we'd put on a palm-leaf "show" and sing *Ramona* so our parents would clap.

With all sorts of cousins, in the houses of both grandparents, we performed. While the parents sat and talked or finished their dinners, we youngsters would always put together a show. Grandmother Allison's house had sliding doors between the front hall and the living room, which made it perfect for a stage.

My youngest sister Mary wound up being the star every time because she was smaller in stature to begin with, she was the spoiled baby on both sides of the family, and she was enormously talented for a little kid. She'd fling on a feather boa and imitate Mae West, or she'd go into her Shirley Temple tap-dance routine. The rest of us would recite pieces or sing trios or some such. The parents always applauded, of course.

Both "sides" of our family had musical talent. Aunt Jim or Aunt Bess would play the Allison piano. My mother played the violin. My dad fancied himself quite a singer. Aunt Vera specialized in *The Maple Leaf Rag*. Aunt Millie, on Mother's side, would play *The Big Tin Pan Parade* while we all marched around and around Grandad's house beating on pans and buckets. All of us loved to perform, so it's strange that not one professional performer emerged from the tribe. Close as we came to professional was Aunt Bess playing the organ for the Presbyterian Church.

Popular songs in the '20s and '30s spread across the country

slowly. Some we heard from Ruby Keeler and other musical movies, but most came to us from the radio and from sheet music. Records had only one song on each side—no albums, except some of the classical music from Red Seal. But we managed to learn the lyrics of almost every song that came along.

Our best source for songs, words and music, always was Aunt Jim. (She had that name because she was the sixth girl before my dad was born, and Grandfather just gave up hoping for a boy and named her Jim.) Aunt Jim lived in Los Angeles, so she had access to all of the latest hits. When she arrived in McPherson, unpacking the new sheet music and playing and singing the new songs held highest priority.

Once in a while the grownups would insist on being a part of our act. My dad particularly loved to recite *The Hermit of Sharktooth Shoal*, which he claimed Robert Service had written. The only line I recall to this day was, "He cast a smirch on the Baptist Church when he betrayed a girl named Ruth." Through many years since, we have all heard, read and learned to love many Service poems about Sam McGee and those boys, but never has any of us run into anyone but Dad who recited *The Hermit of Sharktooth Shoal*. But he gave his all in those recitations.

Such was life within our family. We entertained each other, admired each other, perhaps, and lived life to its fullest, Kansas style.

♣

3
WE'LL PACK OUR "THESE AND THOSIES"

Kansans travel. At least, most of them do. We grew up well aware of the endless plains around us. But we knew of mountains and beaches and national parks. Kansans have more of a tendency to see the rest of the world than those folks who live in some self-styled paradise. Therefore, you will find more Kansans who have seen Mount Rushmore and Cape Cod and Butchart Gardens than Californians, let's say. This theory I made up myself, of course, but per capita, I'd bet on it.

The majority of our neighbors, friends and relatives vacationed either in Minnesota or Colorado. Because of our Grandad Jensen, we vacationed more in California. Eventually, we had a second home at Balboa. My earliest recollections of traveling to California were on the train. We loved those trips. Mother boarded the Santa Fe *Chief* with four little girls, the youngest still a babe in arms, and we had one high old time all the way to San Bernardino.

It took us no time to settle into our section and get acquainted with other passengers as we ran around the cars being our cute little selves. We discovered fellow travelers with huge baskets who gave us bananas and offered to hold the baby for Mother. We knew how to order in the dining car and how to climb into the upper berths. Mother might have been frantic looking for us once in a while, but it had to be a much more relaxed way to get to Grandad's than flying like today's families, all strapped into our seats, or driving and fighting over who gets to sit by the window.

When Dad could come along we did drive out, rumbling across gravel roads on Route 66, fighting flat tires and boiling radiators and the heat of the desert. On the road we either slept, fought, or sang. We memorized Burma Shave signs and sometimes played alphabet with billboards. Our parents sang a lot, too. We must have known 500 songs or more, from their old favorites like *Yes, Sir, That's My Baby* to songs of the '20s and '30s: *Shuffle Off to Buffalo* and *Blue Skies*.

Mother has always been germ-conscious. Her middle name should have been Lysol. Every trip was interrupted at crucial moments while Mother sterilized toilet seats from Garden City, Kansas, to Blythe, California.

Once, in Grants, New Mexico, before 66 was even a paved road, we stopped for the night at one of the first-ever "cabin camps." Nobody could have been as happy to see those "modern facilities" as I was. I leaped out of that '30 Buick dancing on one foot and then the other while Dad unlocked the door to our cabin, but Mother dashed in ahead of me with the Lysol. I presume my sisters followed in like urgency. (Dad stopped along the road only for gas or cigarettes.) Because of the rush, I suppose, Mother used Lysol full strength on the toilet seat.

Gratefully, I made it just in time, but when I stood up all of the paint on that seat came with me, stuck to my seat, as it were. Mother dumped me in the tub before the Lysol could blister. We left that place in record time in the morning before the proprietor discovered Mother's over-zealous handiwork.

Crossing the desert in a car before air conditioning tested the traveler beyond any torture generally practiced in families today. If the Joads had had air conditioning, the *Grapes of Wrath* might never have been written. That desert air burned. Eventually we had air conditioners that attached to the window of the car. These hollow cylinders lined with excelsior had to be kept wet with water from the canvas bag hanging from the door handle. The person seated right next to the window enjoyed a moist breeze while the rest of the group yelled about getting out of the way "so we can get some of the cool air." But we read comic books and sang songs and begged Dad to stop for a cream soda. Since station wagons had not yet been invented, we rode on jump seats in a seven-passenger sedan. Some way, that gave us more to fight about.

Once, we turned our sights eastward. Our parents felt we ought to see The East. These were junior high days for me. Such an extensive trip took endurance and time on the part of our parents.

We saw Springfield, Illinois, just after Abraham Lincoln's home had closed for the day.

We peered into Mount Vernon through locked gates just after the guards had swung them shut.

In short, we missed touring hours all the way from Kansas through New England, including the chance to go to the top of the Washington Monument.

Our father had the attitude that once you've seen the outside, you can read about the rest. Not only did he refuse to stop unless he needed gas or cigarettes, he clung loyally to that all-male theory that asking for directions shows weakness on the part of any real man. So we sang and slept a lot more while Mother and Dad discussed directions and distances for miles on end. Dad's favorite saying: "There's got to be a better place for lunch on the other side of this town." I'll bet you've heard that one, too.

New Mexico vacations always turned up something special. Red River, New Mexico, in the early '30s was nothing more than a peaceful, cool, mountain valley with a mountain stream, two inns and a grocery store. Kansans and Texans shared the joys of Red River, where we hiked, had picnics, rode battered old horses, and went over to Eagle Nest to fish. Predictably, Red River provided such an idyllic time that it has grown out of all proportion and the charm has been transformed to New Mexico glitz, whatever that might be. But we loved it.

One day in Red River, we talked our dad into renting horses for a trail ride. I must have been about ten years old. Ann, at eleven, chose the horses we wanted, but we came up one short: No horse for Dad.

Ann and I spotted a horse that seemed just right for our dad in a separate corral. The man refused—said that horse hadn't been well-enough "broke" for tourists. Having heard many stories of the wonders our father could do, we insisted our dad could ride anything. Dad had to admit he was no Tom Mix or get on the snorting beast. On he went, and the horse headed straight for the general store where he jumped up on the porch and proceeded to buck like crazy under the tin roof. Dad hit the roof, then he landed on the horse, then he hit the roof again, then the horse, until some way he managed to dismount. Our ride was postponed—indefinitely.

One of the tragedies of our young lives hit in Red River. We were absolutely devoted to Will Rogers. Some of our cousins lived in Claremore, Oklahoma, Rogers's home town. When I was five, my dad introduced me to Will Rogers on the street in Salina, Kansas. My hero shook my hand. Obviously, I never forgot that. The fifteen minutes when Will Rogers talked on the radio ranked in importance even above *Amos 'n' Andy*. We never missed one of his movies: *State Fair* with Janet Gaynor, and all the rest.

On that day in August, 1935, we heard the news of that plane crash in Alaska while walking down the street of Taos. Driving back to Red River, we kept the car radio on, hoping against hope for news of a rescue. There in that place, that accident became a personal tragedy for us and for everyone around.

One of my own sons remarked years later, "If you want to make Mom cry, just mention Will Rogers."

New Mexico holiday memories will forever bring back to me the image of my red-haired sister Ann, about 12 years old, at a campfire in Red River. The m.c. of the evening invited any of us tourists to get up and perform. Ann stood up and sang *I'll Never Say Never Again Again*, swinging her adolescent hips and snapping her fingers while I very nearly died. Then Mary, the little show-off of the family, did her Betty Boop impersonation followed by her Mae West impression minus the boa. Growing up in that family with any dignity was tough sometimes.

My sister Ann, in reading early drafts of this journal, has insisted I am all mixed up about this event. Ann claims some other young folks at the campfire sang *I'll Never Say Never Again Again*, but it's her word against mine. I could swear Ann sang that song that night, and if that turns out to be the only mistake I've made in recording these memories, we can call it a miracle.

ᘓ

Red River days faded in frequency after we had the houses at the beach. As we grew into junior high and high school, our parents first rented, then bought, a house on the peninsula at Balboa, which we shared with the California branches of our family. As little kids, we had worn those smashing outfits known as beach pajamas—wild, printed one-piece jobs with wide legs and matching hats. Those gave way, happily, to more sophisticated beachwear, concentration on acquiring a great tan, and, in 1943, the arrival of new neighbors at our house.

The Army Air Corps rented the house next to ours as a rescue station for fliers in trouble over the ocean from the base at Santa Ana. Can you imagine anything grander for my sisters, cousins, and me than living all summer next to all those cute guys in their darling fatigues, waiting for a call to pick up some pilot from the drink off Newport Beach? Most of the war was tough, but that part we thoroughly enjoyed.

World War II put an end to California vacations and beach houses, eventually. Along with that came ration stamps, bandage-rolling, V-mail, excruciating headlines of Bataan and Corregidor, blue and gold stars in the windows of our neighbors, college without guys, bond drives, leg makeup, oleomargarine, Spam, and the rest of our lives—never to be the same.

❧

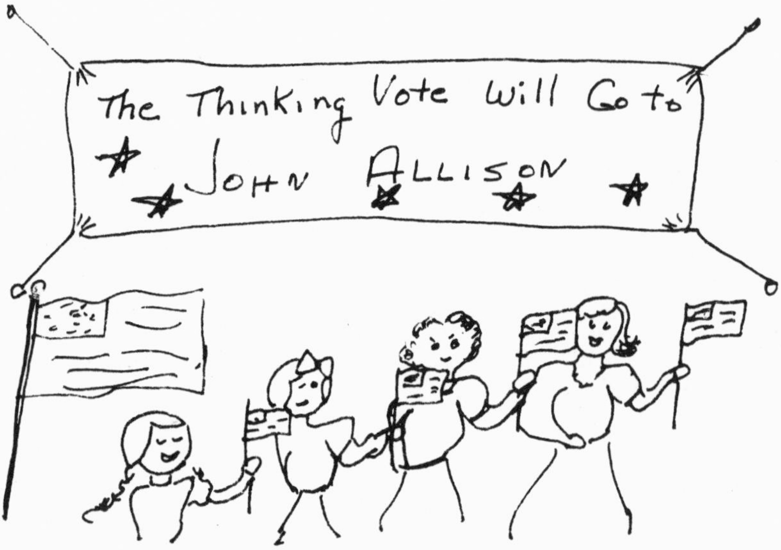
The Thinking Vote Will Go to
JOHN ALLISON

4
IT'S NOT WHERE YOU START . . .

That pretty well covers McPherson days. Scenes of small town childhood. Since beginning this treatise, more and more memories have reconstructed themselves in my brain. If I try to include the man in the horse-drawn wagon who sold us ice cream cones and licked the spoon or our picnics on Coronado Heights, the highest point in McPherson County (100 feet?), I'd never get on to the rest of the story.

Should I try to point out the thousands of instances of "progress" that have passed through my mind on this journey through the late '20s to the mid-'40s, I'd have to mention the wonder drugs and detergents and automatic washers. I'd be tempted to recall being able to read the headlines in the *McPherson Daily Republican* about Pretty Boy Floyd and John Dillinger. I'd have to explain again to my children why we wore woolen swim suits and silk stockings; why women wore heavy corsets and we kids laughed at ads about "before I got my Spencer . . ." Someone would surely ask about begging chips of ice from the back of the delivery wagon on a summer day. Rumble seats and running boards on Packards and LaSalles or my dad's Studebaker roadster with red leather seats and wire wheels would come up sooner or later.

What, or who, emerged from all of this? Four women now in our 60s who share more than anything else a deep family loyalty, an appreciation of the good Life as we perceive it, faith in ourselves and each other.

Never far from the surface lurks the sense of humor in all of us that has kept us laughing since the days when Dad used to "brag" about Ann, telling his friends,

"When Ann was only twelve, I could say her name and she'd turn around. Just like that!"

Dad got it back from our youngest sister Mary when it came to quick retorts. In the midst of regaling friends about his escapades at a Republican convention, where he had posed as a newspaper reporter, Dad claimed, "I'd strut up to one of those pompous politicians and say, 'I'm Allison from the *Times*.'"

Eight-year-old Mary Marn, sitting next to Dad, stuck out her hand.

"I'm Brown from the *Sun*."

Mary got the big laugh, of course, and our generally genial father pouted the rest of the evening.

My younger sister Middy, third on the line, pointed out to me in her perusal of this manuscript that I had not mentioned her—at least not as much as I had oldest Ann and youngest Mary.

"Neither have I written a lot about what I was doing," I replied. "We're middle kids." The longer I live, the more I believe in the effects of birth order in our lives.

Education was of prime importance. All of my father's six older sisters had graduated from college, which amazes me in speaking of young women at the turn of the century. My parents and my Mother's sister also had college educations. It was assumed we'd finish college back in those days when parents' assumptions were seldom questioned. We saw ourselves not as the intelligencia, for heaven's sake; we just went to college.

∽

Now about politics. In our early days in Kansas, all political discussions around our house had to be pro-Republican. Not that we ever thought Landon would win in '36, but we had some heavy Republican background from Grandfather Allison. One of the embarrassments of my young life was the fact that my California grandfather was a

Democrat. I was happy he lived so far away. He liked the New Deal. We couldn't understand that.

Mother actually began our family involvement in government. During our public-school days, our mother served several terms on the school board. That made life a lot easier, once in a while. Other times, it was a pain in the neck. Some teachers, like Miss Brooks in home ec, would give me an A for anything because my mother was . . .

When it came time for any sort of horseplay, the fact that our mom would be the first to hear about it kept all four of us in line. Mother did a good job. Her name still shines on the plaque on the new high school in McPherson, which is now the old high school.

In 1942 my father challenged Senator Arthur Capper for the Republican nomination for Capper's seat in the U. S. Senate. What an exciting summer that was! Capper had been in the Senate for four terms already. He was in his 70s. Now that I'm in my 60s, that doesn't seem so bad. But in 1942, with the war going badly and Capper's continuing isolationist attitude and pronouncements an embarrassment to all of us more progressive Republicans, Dad's principal campaign centered on the need for younger, stronger, leadership from Kansas in Washington.

Dad was right, of course, but he didn't win. Close, but no cigar.

We rallied 'round old Dad with a vengeance, trying to type campaign letters, delivering posters and leaflets. Ann went along on some of the trips around the state and had her picture in the paper grinning at Dad and saying all the right things. We all had our pictures taken for publicity photos, mostly of the four of us and Mother gazing rapturously at the flag flying in our own front yard.

Ann and I transferred to Kansas State College so Our Candidate wouldn't have to face the embarrassment of having sent his daughters to out-of-state schools. That decision, looking back, apparently did nothing to win the election. All it affected was the rest of our lives. Instead of moving to Washington, we took the bus to Manhattan, Kansas, joined the Pi Phis, and lived happily ever after.

Among my souvenirs I have the scrapbook of the Allison-for-Senate campaign I made for Dad. Before the incontestable impact of TV on politics, newspaper coverage carried the most clout. Radio amounted to something, but not like the papers.

The most respected newsman in Kansas was William Allen White of the *Emporia Gazette*. The *Gazette* stood behind Capper against John Allison, but White had this to say about my father:

> *[In the Gazette] no unkind word will be said about John Allison. He is a handsome, forthright, straight-talking, apparently square-shooting young Republican. His open brown eyes look you in the face unflinchingly. He is not afraid to say something you don't like. No pollyfoxer is John Allison. Certainly he is no crank, no crackpot, no dreamer. He is master of his own soul. Arthur Capper need not fear a foul fight. John Allison will not hit below the belt. He is a decent and worthy foe. Allison also is one of the men who, in the next 30 years in this state, is bound to make his impress on Kansas, whether in politics or in business.*

In the long run, business interested Dad more than public office, so he never tried running for anything again. My sisters and I, however, enjoyed involvement in politics later on and so did our husbands.

❧

Kansas families had their hard times but the work ethic ruled. My father nearly died in a cave-in of a ditch he had contracted. Twenty-seven tons of dirt piled in on Dad after he had cleared the workmen from the site to test the braces himself.

Later, Dad and his first partners in the business of distributing natural gas spent below-zero nights out with the regulator valves to maintain constant pressure to serve the needs of communities converting to natural-gas furnaces. Their fledgling company could not afford automatic pressure regulators on their newly laid gas lines, so these two young men stayed out there all night to make the system go. Of course, they had no heat of their own—not even the smoke from a cigarette, with all that gas around. By the next winter you can bet they had *that* problem solved. From that time on, my dad's part of the business was promotion. Somebody else kept the gas going. The business flourished and my parents moved to Colorado three years after the summer of '42.

Dad's example and enthusiasm were not wasted on us, either in business or in politics. We all made more of a mark on the political scene, however. Only one of us, Ann, has made much a mark in the world of commerce. Real estate.

Middy served as president of the Colorado Federation of Republican Women, among other campaign jobs. I started out being a city councilman in Prairie Village (suburban Kansas City) and wound up vice-chairman of the Republicans in Pueblo, Colorado. Ann and Mary have participated, usually when we made up campaign songs, blew up balloons, or tried to convince somebody—anybody—to buy tickets to the Republican barbecue in Pueblo, a Steelworkers town. Usually we wound up singing.

It's hard to tell which campaign song we liked best. We sang about Thomas Dewey to the tune of *The Missouri Waltz*. One line, "We've one leg to stand on / He's better than Landon," shall live forever in the musical annals of the family. Later came our adaptation of *Davey Crockett* to JFK:

> *Born in Massachusetts with a silver spoon,*
> *Joe said we'll run him for office soon.*
> *Sent him off to Harvard and his mamma said,*
> *If he doesn't win, we'll try Bobby or Ted.*
> *There goes Little Johnny, headin' for his New Frontier.*

How long ago even that seems, now.

Back to the music part: For all of the time and energy spent in music lessons and forced practice hours, we should have some accomplished musicians in my generation, but such did not happen. Ann and I started lessons on the piano at ages five and six, I'd guess. Miss Fern Lingenfelter taught in her studio above the butcher shop on Main Street. We had private lessons on weekdays, class lessons on Saturday mornings.

After class lesson, we had to go into the butcher shop to call Mother to come get us. I just hated that. Ann made me go because the man scared her. Well, that butcher scared me, too, but at five or six years old I had no desire to walk home.

By the time Middy, two years younger than I, had reached piano-lesson age, we were really in for it. Miss Fern decided we could play trios. Big deal. Ann played the bass, I played the upper end, and Middy sat in the middle, wiggling her butt until she almost pushed Ann and me off the bench. Then she'd play her middle part. But not without

speeding up or slowing down as the spirit moved, so we were never together and Middy always finished first.

We did better when Miss Fern chose marches for us to play, but those recitals devastated Ann and me to the point of considering strangling our dear little sister.

To make matters worse, we had to wear matching outfits. Plaid skirts and white *middy* blouses. Wouldn't you know that Middy'd win?

Most of the time we preferred singing. We would have musicales when Mother played her violin, I played the piano, and the rest of them sang, or we all just sang. We sang in the car. We sang doing the dishes. We sang with the radio. We sang walking down the beach. We sang at parties. We sang harmony or we sang silly songs, but boy, did we sing. Our folks had taught us, at home and riding in the car, the songs of their youth. We all knew *Roses of Picardy* and *The Sunshine of Your Smile.*

We knew the words to most of the hymns, particularly Grandmother's favorite, "And He walks with me and He talks with me . . ." I still picture Grandmother on her front walk, carrying her purse, strolling along with Jesus, when I hear that one.

As teenagers we played records, listened endlessly to the big bands on the radio, and took Benny Goodman's side against the Artie Shaw fans of our world. We could sing any Glenn Miller hit or any song from Ginger and Fred's movies.

Now, here comes the best part: We still know all of those lyrics, my sisters and I. Just name that tune and we're off and running. Don't waste song sheets on the Allison girls. We know 'em all.

Why? How? Lyrics used to be worth memorizing. My father could sing his way through *The Lost Chord* without a mistake for as long as he lived. Youngest sister Mary, who has by far the best voice, could belt out *Ebbtide* to rattle the rafters. Just one word, almost any word, can set Middy humming or whistling some tune we all know.

Of course these days we sing in a much lower range. We sound really weird sometimes, and our families shudder when it looks as if the mothers might tune up, but singing remains a major part of our heritage.

&

I must add one big thing about this family of ours from those Kansas days to this. We join. From the time we first realized our mother went to meetings of the 20th Century Club on Wednesdays and Progressive Literature on Tuesday and our dad talked about being an SAE— whatever that was—my sisters and I believed in and participated in organized social life. So did most of our town.

Ann came home from Roosevelt School fourth grade one day to break the news timidly to Mother that she had been invited to join a club of older girls. It seems to me it was a sewing club, and Martheda Johnson had asked Ann to become a member. As soon as Ann acted willing to accept such an honor, Martheda said, "Good, kid. We'll have our next meeting at your house." Mother, as I recall, vetoed Ann's election to the club.

My two younger sisters, Middy (for Mildred) and Mary Marn (for Mother) shared the pink bedroom. Ann and I had the blue one. About the time these two little girls started to school they had their own clubs. After lights out at 7:30 or 8:00, we could hear them discussing their latest club—usually electing officers. Middy must have been six or seven, Mary four or five. We eavesdropped on their haggling during their meetings in the darkened bedroom.

Said Middy, "We will be the Busy Bee Sewing Club. Good. Now we elect officers."

Said Mary, "This time I want to be the president."

Middy's answer never varied. "Now, Mary Marn, just think about this. This club should have a president who is older and knows more about clubs. You can be the vice-president. And you can be the secretary, too. Then you'll have two offices but I'll have just one."

Mary Marn: "That's just like our last club. I hate being the vice-president and the secretary."

Middy: "Okay. You can be the vice-president and treasurer."

And off they went to sleep.

It grieves me to add that years later when these sisters were in their fifties, our only serious family conflict about money came up and Mary (still the youngest) blurted out to me:

"Okay. Okay. I'm still the baby sister. I never will get to be president of the club!"

Isn't that sad? And we thought they were so cute. You never know about kids.

On a happier note, we can discuss the Sub-Deb Club. When Ann and I went to junior high, the *Ladies Home Journal* featured a page for teen-agers with hints about clothes, complexion, manners, boys, all that. Through the magazine's sponsorship girls all over the country formed local Sub-Deb Clubs. I belonged with Ann's class. We met on Saturdays and talked over program and study materials sent from the *Journal.*

We also learned community service. On Sunday mornings in the summer two of us Sub-Debs fixed flowers in little vases to deliver to the patients in the McPherson hospital. We had dances and teas and discussed every known subject except sex.

Our very best club in the family from pre-teen years until we became Pi Phis and Delta Gammas had only six members: two California cousins and the four of us. The Gibson Girls. One of the boys who hung around our cute blonde cousins in Redlands was Bobby Gibson. Bobby gossiped about every one in town. He knew it all. The gossip from Bobby Gibson filled our lazy summer days with some spice, but we did wonder what sort of tales he was telling about us.

Our own secret society for telling secrets had to be named the

Gibson Girls. We went all out on this one. Our motto was, "An eye to the keyhole, an ear to the ground. Be prepared . . . to run." We had specially made gold-and-black pins with two G's in a diamond shape. The guard on the chain was crossed keys. I still have mine.

For years we had GG meetings whenever we gathered for summer vacations at the beach. Middy was always the president. You could have guessed that. Mary was the messenger. She had to run to ask our folks for money for the movies and such. The rest of us were spies. One cardinal rule of membership: If you know a secret you must tell it to the other "Gibbies." You also were honor-bound to answer any questions from the other members.

Best of all, the Gibson Girls had ceremonies. The Toast to Balboa Bay ended every summer even after we had gone off to college and were headed for lives of our own. In the Fun Zone at Balboa all of us and our mothers loved the Grunt Derby. Mechanical pigs raced around a track propelled (apparently) by balls rolled to drop into holes by the contestants. You rolled your ball to the right hole, your pig moved along the track.

We saved our winning tickets from the Grunt Derby (back in the late '30s, this was) to claim an ugly ceramic decanter and a set of small cups. Might have been intended for saké, but what did we know? Those cheap brown vessels became our sacred wine set. Every year on our last beach night the Gibson Girls would sneak out of the house to the waterfront at 2 a.m., fill our decanter with ginger ale, and drink our toast to the bay.

Frivolous? Certainly. But those girlhood bonds still hold us in a very secret way. Naturally we all joined in community affairs and organizations, although much of that has been turned over to younger women by this time. They like being president.

Our children learned early about being in families of joiners. When Chris, our No. 1 son, was about three, my dad bought an Angus calf for each of his grandchildren and enrolled them in the Junior Angus Breeders Association. Chris asked immediately if this could be anything like P.E.O. and when could he go to the meetings.

So there you have it, folks. My childhood and teen years as I recall: basically pleasant, warm and safe. It took me six months to recover from a ruptured appendix, but recover I did. Fewer of us wore braces or ate broccoli. In looking back over those long-gone days when chicken pox meant a sign on your house and polio ran rampant, it's the details that fill in the picture. Our lives, of my family and me, fit the pattern of mid-American middle-class morality. Who couldn't grow up "happy" under such circumstances? We lived in such a stable community we actually studied under some of the same teachers who had taught our parents. Everyone in town was our friend.

Meanwhile, we girls had the expected gripes:

Mother wouldn't let us wear lipstick to school.

Mother wouldn't allow us to hang around Hubbell's much.

Mother made us wear winter underwear 'til Easter.

Mother didn't let us drive as soon as our friends did.

Mother wouldn't let us call up the boys.

Mother always knew when we tried to smoke.

Mother never really trusted any of us, including Dad.

She still doesn't.

❧

5
ONE KID AFTER ANOTHER

Allison felt just awful.

Five years old, a kindergartener at Prairie School, she had been brought home by the school nurse. Some flu bug had laid her low. Her mother had gone to some sort of a meeting, as usual. Poor sick waif had only the cleaning lady to comfort her. Lucinda turned on the TV while Allison settled herself on the couch with a handful of Oreos.

In 1951, TV opened new worlds for Allison. No cartoons. The terminal illness of the British monarch had preempted regular programming. Droning on and on, reporters with British accents detailed every moment of what were assumed to be the last hours of the king's reign. Head aching, hot with fever, throat sore and cookies almost gone, Allison turned her most pitiful look to the maid.

"Well, Lucinda," she croaked, "I guess it's just me and King George."

Allison probably learned many of her lessons about Life and Death on TV. Hers was the first generation to have access to that artificial world during most of their growing years. We soon realized she'd picked up more than we anticipated during those early '50's. The kids of America mixed the messages of the Mousketeers, Buffalo Bob, and *I Love Lucy* with assorted newscasts about Christine Jorgensen and other sensational medical "miracles."

Allison and Chris, who must have been five and three, played all sorts of make-believe in their basement playroom. I had a tough time getting anything done upstairs because I'd perch on the top step, out of sight, just to listen to these games.

"Say, Judy," Chris said one day (I'm not sure who "Judy" was), "Did you know Lucy—*I Love Lucy*—did you know I Love Lucy had a baby?"

"Did I know it?" Allison shouted. "Did I know it? I was right there when she had that baby. It took nine Danish doctors to decide if it was a girl or a boy!"

♋

It came as no surprise to me that we had funny children. From the first time I visited the Weaver household in Concordia, Kansas, I understood that mixing the Allison and Weaver penchants for a good laugh would make for more than a few chuckles along the way. Our family has laughed through a lot.

John and I met in our first weeks at Kansas State. Nineteen forty-two. I had transferred from Colorado College in Colorado Springs as a sophomore. John played freshman football, became an SAE, and made fine grades in pre-med for six months at Manhattan before the enlisted reserves were called up and he took off for parts unknown. He, John Weaver, had accomplished one more feat. He had managed to fall in love, and so had I.

What a guy he was. He was an athlete, a scholar, and a born leader. In Concordia John had made all-conference or whatever in his football years, had set state records swimming in competitions when he was the only member of the Concordia team, had been president of his class forever, had played the lead in *Our Town,* had been the lifeguard and swim coach ever since he was 13 or 14 years old, and was generally the town hero. He was also a barrel-chested, fit, trim blonde who looked awfully good to this lovesick McPherson girl.

I used to stand at the window outside my chemistry lab on Tuesday mornings knowing I'd see John coming out of the library, and if I timed it just right, I'd "run into" him on the campus. We'd meet not really by chance, as the song said.

Sorority hours were strictly enforced in those days. We spent precious moments huddled into the darkest corner available on the side porch of the Pi Phi house. Only a few students had cars in those war years; we walked and settled for what privacy we could find, even though snuggling on the Pi Phi porch was not unlike smooching in front of your mother.

Life in the early '40s still stuck to the old Victorian ideals of love and marriage. Can't have one without the other. When you "did it," you had "had it." No fooling around or experimenting; once was enough to seal the commitment. 'Til death do us part.

We lived by that credo. Some marriages may have been made in heaven. Ours was made in the back seat of Earl Hunter's old Ford on a cold March night on a country road near Manhattan, Kansas. The moon was full, shining on crusty snow.

The next morning, John reported to Fort Leavenworth. The enlisted reserves had been called to active duty. John's days as a Kansas Aggie came to a sudden halt, but our lives had just begun. We knew then, just as we knew almost forty years later when John died, that we had sealed the bargain right there and then. Forever. Not the world's best marriage nor the worst, but we stayed together and stuck it out the best we knew how.

John reported as ordered to Fort Leavenworth, then on to Fort Belvoir in the Engineers, to Georgetown for testing, thence to the City College of New York for pre-med, which he finished in 18 months.

John Weaver was the only man I know who served in the army for three solid years and never made PFC. Never did he rise above buck private. But he got his pre-med among the best in the country, served at Indiantown Gap while waiting for medical school at Jefferson in Philadelphia, and was half-way through his freshman year in med school before his discharge in March, 1946.

Those years I spent in Manhattan, Kansas, finishing my own med-tech education and writing letters. John and I wrote to each other every day. Once in a great while, he'd come home on furlough and I'd spend that time in Concordia with John and his folks. Concordia was just McPherson with hills.

We were engaged by the end of my junior year and married soon after my graduation. Our entire courtship, for all practical purposes, had been on paper. We fell in love, sealed the deal, wrote letters, got married. Then we got acquainted.

Many marriages of those days followed the same pattern. On the campus at Kansas State men were rare as hen's teeth. Since it was an ag college, there might actually have been more hen's teeth there than guys. This condition reflects in my post-college years. We formed much closer friendships with the other girls in the house during the war years than we would have otherwise. We depended on each other more, competed with each other less without the scurry of dating as a way of life. Those college friends are still some of my favorite people.

∽

On my first visit to the Weaver household in 1943, John's dad came home for lunch from the post office absolutely convulsed over some clerk in the court house who had accidentally stapled his own finger to his desk. The family laughed and laughed.

From his vantage point on the life of Concordia through his window in the post office, Joe Weaver usually brought home some sort of a joke. His favorite:

"Did you hear about the man who decided his wife would look good in something long and flowing, so he dumped her in the Mississippi River?"

Wartime marriages, wartime weddings, had to be different than we had expected in our youth. John could be home on furlough in

early July after my graduation, so the date was set. July 3, 1945. Traditional gifts like sterling silver place settings had gone the way of Lucky Strike Green and real butter. I was married in a rayon dress with none of the showers today's brides find so necessary and only those guests who could manage to get to our parents' new home in Colorado. We received seven sets of bookends and twelve bent glass trays.

Why I was not married in Kansas I wondered years later, but in wartime we often made it harder on ourselves just trying to keep the old (normal?) ways intact.

Nothing seemed normal for me about moving for two months to Lebanon, Pennsylvania, to live among the Pennsylvania Dutch until med school started in September. John left for the base every morning early and I spent my days delighting in being among people so different from my home folks. When some woman on a street corner remarked to me, "It wonders me if it will make down rain," I ran right to our one-room "apartment" to call my mother to tell her about it. I shopped in the Amish farmers' market and we ate Lebanon baloney for almost every meal. A new world lay before me, a joy I have never lost whenever confronted by "strangers."

Philadelphia provided more challenges and more adventures for John and me. We had one helluva time finding a place to live. Housing for buck privates listed with the housing units of the USO or whatever looked and smelled like the places Kansans would keep their pigs. Finally one nice lady volunteer took pity on us and let us peek into the housing file for officers. We found one room for light housekeeping in a century-old row house at 13th and Spruce Streets, about six blocks from the Jefferson Medical College in the wondrous old section of downtown Philadelphia. Fine. I found a job as a lab technician at the medical school in the department of pharmacology and we were all set.

Too often we recall opportunities bypassed with regret. Not so with our first days in Philadelphia, as far as I'm concerned.

One of the professors who interviewed me for a lab job decided I, too, should be in medical school. Since Jefferson at that time did not admit women, this kind man arranged that I might become a medical student at Temple University. He even managed to get the admission for me.

On the day I was to report to Temple University, I threw up for the first bout of morning sickness. Allison was on her way. No way would I go to medical school. Not in those days.

That opportunity was bypassed, certainly, but I have never regretted for one minute not becoming a doctor. John and I created enough competition without that during our marriage. But more important, I have loved being just Mother. Housewife never sounded like a dirty word to me. One job sufficed when the kids were little, and I found satisfaction enough in my sideline: being the most enthusiastic volunteer west of any given point for more than 30 years.

I don't want to pass the Philadelphia days without giving you a real idea of our first housing. We had one big room at the back of the third floor of this old row house, which was only one room wide to begin with. The landlady had a Doberman so fearsome I had to wait to walk home with John because I was afraid to open the front door. Besides, we had to buy groceries on the way home every day because we had no refrigerator, and I just knew that dog would grab my veal chops before I made it to our own door.

Once inside, we had to plan cooking carefully. Our kitchen had been the closet. Pots, pans and dishes were stored in drawers facing the stove. An ordinary lavatory served as our sink. The trick was to get out all necessary utensils and crockery before turning on the oven. Otherwise, you'd bend over to get whatever you needed and wind up burning your rear end on the oven door. A tight squeeze that was, especially when I was trying to fix oatmeal and John was trying to shave at that sink at the same time.

Aside from that, and the fact that the slats kept falling out of the bed in the middle of the night, and the bathroom was one flight down the dark stairway, we honestly liked living there. John had a good table and lamp for study. I sat at the other end of our big room every evening and tried my hand at needlework, making baby clothes and embroidering a Farmer-in-the-Dell quilt for the baby. We referred to our expected infant as "Navajo," since everyone has heard of the Navajo Weavers.

Our first crisis came in this first year of medical school. About five months' pregnant, I had been working in research on new pain-killer drugs using dogs that were kept in hospital-clean kennels on the top floor of the school. One of our dogs suddenly turned mean and vicious, then died. An autopsy proved the dog had rabies. Everyone in the department would have to take the Pasteur treatment since we had all handled the dog.

My obstetrician said "no way." Since this man was the head of the OB department taking care of a student's wife for nothing, we had no desire to argue the point, but rabies scared John and me. During the next two weeks I spent my days listening to my fellow workers complaining about the terrible shots that I could not take, then each evening, thinking rabies, John and I made a list of all the people I was going to bite.

Allison arrived right on schedule, none the worse for the dog scare. We went to Concordia to await her arrival in June of 1946, one year of medical school behind us.

My mother had been beside herself at the thought of her daughter going through the "agony of childbirth." She referred to having babies in only those terms.

John's mother was more casual. "Well, we all live through it," she'd comment whenever I expressed fears about the coming events.

On the morning after delivery of my firstborn I had to admit to John, "It wasn't nearly as bad as my mother said it would be, but it was a helluva lot worse than *your* mother said."

In those days, those two weeks in the hospital turned us all into weakened caricatures of our former selves by the time we got home and took charge of our offspring. But we all survived, including the grandmothers.

My worst job during John's school years turned out to be "holding the book." I had had courses in anatomy, physiology, bacteriology, biochemistry and such in getting my degree. Hence, I should have been able to quiz John as he faced these subjects. From the beginning he knew more than I did, or he made me feel that he did, so some of those sessions where I supposedly quizzed him in preparation for a test left us a bit testy ourselves. He'd come up with a 98 or so no matter what I did, so I stopped worrying about it. My knowledge of anatomy actually did help in his learning the origins and insertions of muscles and the topography of the nervous system—or at least he said it did.

Summers during medical school were spent with our families. As a matter of fact, John and I had been married for four years before we had a home to ourselves. We divided summers evenly between Concordia and Colorado Springs, six weeks each. Both sets of parents put up with us and the two children we had by the time John had that precious degree and we had used up the GI Bill.

My parents lived on a ranch north of Colorado Springs where the little kids could swim and fish and sometimes ride the pony. At the

Weavers the chickens in the back yard and the wonderful vegetable garden kept them occupied. Joe Weaver doted on his tomatoes more than any man I've known. More than anything, Joe and Vesta loved to take the children for a ride. They would take off down the road to Glasco or some other town close by with Vesta singing and the kids shouting whenever Joe took a little hill fast enough to bounce a bit. When Vesta decided Joe was driving too fast, she'd sing out, "Nearer my God to Thee," the kids would squeal, and Joe would slow down for a while.

In the summer of 1947, when Allison could barely pull herself up tall enough to reach the gas jets with white handles on the Weaver kitchen stove, she drove my mother-in-law Vesta and me to distraction constantly turning on the burners. That old stove spouted gas like crazy in the days before automatic pilot lights.

Vesta and I were "reasoning" with the kid. "No, no, Allison," Vesta would say. "Burnie burn! Burnie burn!"

Joe stood this enlightened approach to discipline as long as he could. Marching into the kitchen, he picked Allison up, shook her a bit, and shouted, "No, no, Allison. Blowie all to hell!" Allison got the message.

∾

Of course, no Kansans could face raising a family on Spruce, a crowded, treeless street in Philadelphia. In John's second year, we met Meg Myers, a widow who lived in the suburbs who would rent us the privilege of sharing her house during the school years while she worked, her daughter went to college, John commuted to Jefferson, and I kept our children and took care of the cooking and housework.

Once again, laundry and wringers and clotheslines loomed large in my life. Who can forget the diaper days when we soaked the soiled ones, went through the old Maytag routine, then tried any of a dozen recommended ways of folding?

I had one big trouble at Meg Myers's house. The washer was in the basement, as usual. I'd be down there filling the washing machine, the baby would cry, I'd run upstairs, take care of the kid, and race back down to discover the water had overflowed so I had to mop the floor. Then start on the rinse tubs, remember I had no formula prepared, rush up to start that while the tubs overflowed, so I had to mop the floor some more. Generally after that I would be chatting with the neighbors as we all hung out the diapers and remember the water was running in the rinse tub again. Back to the mop.

Our landlady, Meg, commented after three years and two babies that she'd never seen anyone who kept a laundry room floor as spotless as I did. I smiled and told her I'd learned about doing the laundry from my grandmother. Actually, Mother had also let us help once in a while, but she was much more particular, so we practiced piano lessons while Mother washed.

Just thinking about mopping the laundry room floor reminds me of the abundance of new products appearing almost every day in the late '40s. Meg and I delighted in experimenting with Dreft for dishes, except Meg couldn't get used to the dishwater not feeling soapy. Best of all, we found Spic and Span. Wow. Whole new worlds of clean opened for us.

Without Meg Myers, I don't know what John and I would have done. She was loving to Allison and Chris and understanding about John's need to study. When we left Upper Darby at the end of those years headed for Kansas City, internship and residency, leaving Meg and that neighborhood was far more pain than was leaving home in the first place.

During medical school years our social life consisted of fraternity parties occasionally when the few of us wives huddled in one corner and talked about the dates of the single students. Most of the "brothers" remained single until they finished school or internship. They worked hard at becoming doctors, but they also worked overtime at upholding the reputation of medical students as hard-drinking, fast-living individuals. Those parties would curl your hair. So would some of their dates, as I recall.

During one of those beer-keg blasts while the married women sulked in the corner and the good brothers raised Cain in the rest of the fraternity house, some of the boys decided to "water-bag" pass-ersby. This happened right on a busy downtown street—Locust, perhaps. The happy merrymakers filled paper sacks with water to drop on innocents walking under the windows. Before we knew what was transpiring upstairs, the cops had arrived and trundled the good brothers off to the precinct house.

Word came back to the party (still going full force without the waterworks) that the precinct captain studied John's disheveled classmates staggering and dripping before him and announced, "If youse guys is doctors, I'm glad I'm just a cop." Somehow, I have a feeling med students still try to live up to that same reputation.

Social life for me and for the children caused fewer problems. I had met others in my "boat," away from home with very young children, in alumnae meetings of my sorority, the Pi Phis. Almost immediately those girls and I commenced getting together one day a week to drink coffee, have lunch, discuss baby foods and formulas, and talk about life in general while the babies romped on the floor. In the worst weather or the best, we lugged those kids on the trolley or the bus all over Philadelphia in order to have our own good times. Some of my best friends in the '90s are those same gals, even though the children are grown and our grandchildren are already in college.

Allison was nearly three, Chris almost one, when John graduated with honors from Jefferson Medical College. The Weavers drove east for the great event, then we all drove back to Kansas in two cars since my dad had given us a fine new Studebaker Starlite coupe as a

graduation gift. In later years we heard ourselves grousing about our parents for myriad trivial reasons, but their support of all four of us through medical school was absolutely awesome, to put it mildly, and we never forgot it.

❧

6
EVERYTHING'S UP TO DATE . . .

Mother and Dad kept the children in Colorado while I went house-hunting in Kansas City. John had started his internship on the first of July, and we wanted to get situated as soon as possible. The choice of Kansas City General for internship had been entirely John's. I had lovely thoughts of San Francisco or some more glamorous spot, but John knew more about such matters.

Kansas City General Hospital in those days served only charity patients and paid its interns $25 per month. You read that right. But interns in such a hospital learned and experienced far more in hands-on care than in private hospitals that paid more and taught less. Of course, John proved he was right about all that by becoming one of the finest surgeons west of any given point. And I appreciated his choice even more because living in Kansas City will forever remain one of my favorite experiences. Kansas City I shall love always.

My first day of house-hunting reminded me of the lady at the USO in Philadelphia. Nobody had much to offer the wife of an intern. One man, a Nordic prince named Mr. Lund, showed me through some new "town house rentals" just starting in the area. After his sales pitch, he explained to me the policy about rentals.

"We maintain the ratio here that our tenants are paying no more than 20 per cent of their income in rent."

"Just what is your rent, Mr. Lund?"

"One hundred and twenty-five dollars, Mrs. Weaver."

I drew a deep breath. "Well, Mr. Lund, we have you just

backwards there. My husband's monthly income amounts to 20 per cent of your rent."

"How much does your husband make, Mrs. Weaver?"

"Twenty-five dollars a month."

"*Every month?*" Mr. Lund nearly fainted.

"Yes," I said, "But he gets his laundry."

Once more my dad came to the rescue. He "just happened" to have business in Kansas City at that time and took me house-hunting in earnest. With an iron-clad deal with John about repayment as soon as he began his practice, Dad advanced the down payment on our perfect little house in an ideal neighborhood, Prairie Village, and the Weavers settled in to six years at 4206 Prairie Lane. House payments in those long-ago days were $67 a month, and we had just enough GI Bill to get through the first year. Uncle Sam stepped in to make sure that GI Bill extended several more years.

Allison, four years old, had taught herself to print by this time. I have carefully saved one of her best efforts, a note on manila paper written in purple crayon:

Dear Chris,

I do not like you Chris.

Love, Allison

Chris, only two years old, taught himself all sorts of things. Bright kid, he figured out how to tell time so he'd know when he could get up from his nap. Chris had to get out in the yard quickly in those days to play with his friends.

Not only did he play with the O'Brien boys down the block, Chris had his own set of friends none of the rest of us could see.

"Jim and Jimmy and Bill," he told us.

Those guys could cause more trouble asking Chris to turn on the hose or run across the street than could any visible children around. They hung around under his bedroom window at nap-time so Chris couldn't really go to sleep. He just carried on conversations with Jim and Jimmy and Bill.

Allison's ability to write and spell some words challenged Chris. One day this round-faced pink-cheeked cherub stormed into the kitchen.

"I need you to tell me how to spell 'chun'," he announced. He was almost three.

I thought it over. "Chris, I don't know a word, 'chun,' so I'm not sure how to spell it. Where did you hear that word?"

He was exasperated. "It's my name! Don't you know how to spell my name? Chun. I know C-h-r-i-s but my name is Chris Chun. So how do I spell—?"

When I tried to tell him it started with T he left the kitchen in disgust. Mothers just didn't understand.

John had completed only five months of his four-year surgical residency at the General, I had completed eight months of pregnancy with Ross (number three child) when the Korean conflict shifted into high gear and army-educated doctors all over the country received telegrams from Uncle Sam for Christmas.

The man with the yellow envelope rang our doorbell just days before Christmas. Orders to report to Fort Hood before January 1, 1951. I tried to convince myself that they'd let John come home for at least a leave when the baby was due in January, but John's attitude was more realistic.

"We need doctors now in Korea up on the front lines. No lieutenant reporting for duty at Fort Hood will go anyplace but out, Frances. You know that."

I did know that, but I hoped I was wrong. My concerned parents came to stay with the children and me. Dad took John to the airport because I just couldn't do that. Two days later I tried to call John after he had had the chance to call me once from Texas. His unit had already gone. Actually, John went straight to duty as a battalion surgeon. He was the guy on the front lines who sent the wounded back to the M.A.S.H. units.

Two weeks later, on the 18th of January, I took the kids in the car down to the drug store at the corner in Prairie Village. I just ran in for a minute, as all young mothers say. When I came out, just at dusk, I couldn't find the car right away. It sat in the middle of the busy road, traffic dodging around it. My two children I could see waving at me from inside.

I rushed out, cars stopping to let me through. Allison grinned.

"Chris is a really good driver, Mother. We bumped the handle thing and our car rolled backwards, but Chris steered so the cars didn't hit us. One nice man honked and honked. Aren't we proud of Chris, Mother?"

Four and a half years old. And Chris was two. Somehow I drove up the hill to our house, told my parents what had happened, and collapsed in trembling and tears.

The next day Ross came two weeks early. John did not see Ross until he was almost a year old.

❧

Life smoothed out for the four of us after I recovered from the mumps, which I had contracted in the hospital. The games of imagination continued in the basement. Since her dad had started talking surgery, Allison had invented a new role for Chris. She played the nurse, and Chris was Surgeon Roebucks. Honestly. Then they played school. Guess who always had to be the teacher.

Allison would call roll, about five or six names, then, "Christian Weaver."

Chris would say, "Yeah."

"No, no, Christian," his disgusted teacher would say, "You answer 'present or here.'"

Then she'd call the roll again, all five names. When she called, "Christian Weaver," Chris immediately answered, obediently:

"Present or here."

Discussion of roll-calling took most of the morning.

We could not have had a better place to live in those days than Prairie Village. The contrasts of our living arrangements had been remarkable. From one-room "apartments" in Lebanon and Philadelphia we had moved to Meg's on Carol Boulevard in Upper Darby. Highland Park, to be exact. Older houses on tree-lined streets, back yards with clothes lines and trash incinerators, neighbors who seemed to belong there forever—that was Carol Boulevard. Middle-class security, on our GI Bill income, because of the generosity of Meg Myers.

What a difference in Prairie Village. In 1949 the J. C. Nichols Company, developers of the Country Club District in Kansas City, had forged full speed ahead on their building of smaller affordable housing for younger couples, preferably veterans, in their wonderfully planned community just across Mission Road from the elegance of Mission Hills. We managed to buy, with family help and a VA loan, our two-bedroom house of brown shingles with white trim just a block up from the newly constructed shopping center. Most of our neighbors were college graduates, KU and MU. Today, we'd be called "yuppies," I suppose.

That house could have come straight from *Good Housekeeping*. All we had ever dreamed of—full basement, attached garage, wood-burning fireplace, two bedrooms, big yard, nice neighbors, just enough restrictive covenants to make living very pleasant. And we loved Kansas City. The neighborhood looked after our three children and me while John was away and we managed very well.

Only once did I have a real problem during John's absence. I rolled the car. Yep.

One weekend in March I decided I could take the children out to Concordia to visit their Weaver grandparents. Ross must have been two months old. The trip to Concordia had not seemed too long when we had gone out there before, except for the time we had a dumb black cocker spaniel who insisted on sitting on my lap the whole way. I could drive out there with three children.

And I almost could. Someplace on the road west, or perhaps north, of Manhattan, I told the "big kids" (Allison and Chris, four-and-a-half and two-and-a-half) to settle down for a nap in the back seat of our Studebaker Starlite coupe. The baby slept in his basket in the front seat. Nobody had even heard of seat belts, of course.

I turned to make sure the kids in the back seat followed orders only to realize when I looked back that I had run clear off the left side of the road. One frantic attempt to get us back where we belonged rolled the car.

I'll never forget the noise. The entire world seemed to be crashing around me. I yelled at the children to hang on—to what I don't know—and tried desperately to grab the basket or the baby or something. We turned over, landing on the passenger side of the car. Dust was everywhere. Glass was breaking. Even now, 40 years later, I cannot describe how terrible it all felt. The next thing I knew people appeared from nowhere, lifting the children out of the car, telling me to turn off the ignition, offering all sorts of advice and first aid.

First and most important, we were all right. No broken bones, not even any bleeding. Allison and Chris absolutely became "little soldiers," not even whimpering while the passersby took care of them and

I tried to collect my wits. Except for glass splinters in Ross's basket, we escaped untouched. Imagine.

Along came a Trailways bus—the same bus, with the same driver, I had known in my college days. When I saw that one familiar face, I cried. The driver took us back to Manhattan where John's parents picked us up. Never again did I decide I could handle tripping like that. To this day I will not attempt long drives alone or, even worse, with little people in the car.

Poor John must have been in worse shape than I was when he received my letter about the crash. Not only had he fears about having left our children in my dubious care, he had lost the nicest car he had ever owned. As a matter of fact, that had been the *only* car he'd ever owned. Stuck in some tent on the front lines in Korea, John finally found a way to call home to make sure we were all right. The news about the great deal I'd managed on the new Chevy did not boost his morale like I'd hoped it would.

In retrospect—which could be where I'm living these days of writing, Retrospect, Colorado—I figure I must have attempted that drive halfway across the state of Kansas (200 miles) to prove something. Actually, John's parents and I got along all right, but I had no great yearning to see Concordia and the Weavers. I just wanted to do something, I suppose. And I had been warned again and again about distractions of driving with a car full of small children. At 27 years old, I still had to learn that for myself. Believe me, I learned.

೧

John's return from Korea would have been great in a movie. He had called from San Francisco about his arrival time in Kansas City, but John never did get the hang of time zones. And he never trusted the airlines to know what time it was where they were going. Consequently, just about the time I decided to take the rollers out of my hair, bathe the children and head for the Great Homecoming at the airport, up drove a taxi, and John. None of us was ready, but that didn't bother him. The kids screamed, I cried, and John had his first chance to hold the baby, by now about a year old.

Allison, aware of his uniform, was disappointed. She had started kindergarten while her dad was overseas.

"Are you still in the army, Daddy?"

John nodded.

"Well, by the time you get here again, I'll probably be in first grade."

About six months at near-by Fort Riley took care of John's military obligations and recharged our GI Bill, which carried us through the years of residency, since the hospital upped the ante to $250 per month. We didn't live high, but we lived well enough. In the past year when I have watched some of these TV sob sisters interviewing doctors and other reservists called for active duty, wailing about their hardships and the "unfairness" of the system, I want to choke them. The army has been good to us and millions like us.

∽

In Prairie Village I discovered my true mission in life, aside from wife-mother: volunteer. At that point the satisfaction and the great opportunities in voluntarism in the community, the church, and the neighborhood made sense. After Allison and Chris went to school all day, Ross and I covered most of Johnson County, Kansas, for one good cause or another. From the Pi Phis to the Republicans I took on jobs and obligations that filled my life while the kids were in school and John worked his tail off as a surgical resident.

John came home every other night and every other weekend. Even though he was usually dead tired, he wanted to spend "quality time" with his sons. By the time Chris was in first grade and Ross was about three, John invited them to join his club, the Weaver Men and Boys Reading and Resting Society. Those little boys had a mother who raced off to some sort of a meeting every time they turned around. A club of their own suited them. They joined Dad's club gladly.

Meetings were held on our king-size bed on Saturday and Sunday afternoons, every other week. John and his sons would line up, each with a book. John would read aloud for about ten minutes, then direct the boys' attention to their own reading material while he went sound asleep. The first snore signaled time for the kids to race back outside to play while Dad napped. Every one of the members liked the club meetings. Chris even asked Mr. Stephens next door to join the Weaver Men and Boys.

Years later, three-year-old Ross had grown into twenty-one-year-old dad to Jason, but old habits die hard. Jason, bright sober youngster, spent many weekends with John and me in Beulah while his mom and dad were both going to college and working tirelessly besides.

We figured out Ross's hangover from his childhood one day when John said to Ross's son, Jason, "Come on in the house now, Jason. There's going to be a meeting in there."

Jason turned wide blue eyes to his grandfather and explained simply, "Well, you can have a meeting in there if you want to, Pal, but there won't be any little kids there."

So much for third-generation Reading and Resting.

A foot on every ice floe that went by—John assessed my penchant for charitable and community activities that way. I did not differ in this sense from most of my neighbors. We all had busy husbands, young children and limited budgets. We took part wherever and whenever we could.

The library, for instance. Prairie Village had only been built. We barely had schools. We needed a library. Several of us, probably from a PTA meeting, decided to get something going about a library. We had drives to collect donated books. The owner of the men's store in the Village gave us his basement room. One of the builders drew plans for shelving and helped me talk the J. C. Nichols Company developers out of the lumber. Then housewives armed with hammers and nails proceeded to build a library, which volunteers maintained and operated.

Years later the Johnson County Library in Prairie Village occupies its own impressive quarters, but the start made all of us proud. The Village belonged to us. We loved it.

ಌ

My love for the Village went slightly overboard when I let myself be talked into running for the city council. Those old days of politicking with my dad must have had something to do with it. At any rate, after a campaign that consisted of mailing one postcard to each of the registered voters in my ward pointing out that women spent almost twice as much time in our community as men did so there should be a woman on the council—the men worked downtown on the Missouri side—four men ran against me, but I pulled more votes than all of them put together. Block voting, that's called. Woman Power.

My two terms as a councilman I enjoyed tremendously, except for the honeysuckle and the rats.

As far as I know, every back yard in Prairie Village sloped at least a bit to the rear for natural storm drainage. Heavy rains were carried off at once by the small rivers created in our back yards. In one or two areas, natural beds or "dry creeks" ran down the center of the blocks, more scenic than our unadorned back-yard drainage. These creek beds added to the property values, I'd assume, since landscaping made each home a bit different from the neighbors', even if the floor plans matched. Enthusiastic, energetic, ambitious homeowners dressed up their creek banks by planting along the sides. Most of them chose honeysuckle, which grows fast and covers a lot of ground.

Honeysuckle also provides a great little nesting place and home for rats. Some of the young mothers discovered these varmints back where their children played by the "creeks" and marched down to the City Council to raise hell about such a happening in such a prestigious (in our minds) area.

As luck would have it, my Council job was public health.

"You must do something to protect our kids from these ferocious rats!" the women yelled at me all day long on the phone.

"We'll do whatever seems necessary," I assured them.

Experts from the state health department swarmed in, investigating the only problem the Prairie Village City Council had ever had, since the city was only two years old. Specially designed traps, child-proof, were recommended, as well as other bait devices, to which the enraged parents responded by yelling even louder.

"Okay," I finally announced after much consultation with authorities. "The only way to make sure we get rid of the rats without endangering your children in any way is to cut out and remove all of the honeysuckle."

Then you should have heard them! Those irate souls had paid extra for those lots because of the creek. No way would they tear up their—

Here came the discussion of property values, on which every American suburb depends. The controversy raged to the point I heard myself referred to as the Rat Lady of Prairie Village.

In the long run, I wound up going to each rat's nest with a crew of trained trimmers and cutting back the honeysuckle, then setting out tamper-proof baited traps, which did make life safer for a few children but it certainly upset their folks. I've often wondered what happened in those creek beds after we moved.

I can tell you this much: After the hassle about the rats and the hard-fought battle to build a public swimming pool in Prairie Village ("you mean, open to just *anyone?*") from which I emerged victorious but not unbowed, I never, ever, ran for public office again. I love people, but most of them make lousy constituents.

One other problem of my council stint certainly foreshadowed the future.

In 1954, reports came from the undeveloped land out near Shawnee about a sudsy stream. Laughing about crank calls, our committee of three went to the site of the complaint. There, to our astonishment, we stood in the middle of a pasture through which ran a narrow trickle of a stream under a head of suds about six feet deep. Right. A six-foot-high, one-foot-wide, wall of gray suds. Folks in the neighborhood still had septic systems emptying into this rivulet. The wondrous new detergents and their everlasting suds created this effect across several pastures.

What to do?

We took pictures of the mess and raced to call the state health department. The people who lived along the creek happily washed their clothes in the "free suds."

That was my first glimpse of the problems progress can cause.

Years later our "group conscience" woke up to the rest of the damage we are inflicting on our world.

John absolutely loved his residency, his staff, and the time he spent as chief resident during his fourth year at the General. The children thrived in the neighborhood and at Prairie School. I taught Sunday school and worked with the women of the Church and the PTA and the rest until the day finally came: Time to practice surgery. What an exhilarating thought!

During that final year, as the GI Bill sank slowly into oblivion, we were approached by local surgeons to stay in Kansas City to practice,

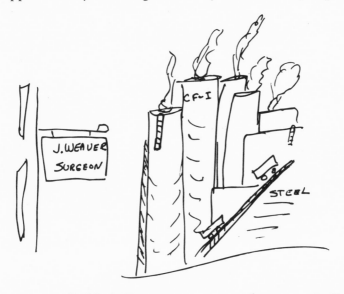

a prospect I really liked. However, two general surgeons in Pueblo, Colorado (the town where my three sisters had snagged husbands and settled down), came around with an offer John just couldn't refuse.

Once more new opportunities, new worlds, and unexpected doors opened for the growing Weaver clan.

പ

After moving to Colorado, we learned to camp.

The travels we girls experienced with our parents certainly contrasted with the tripping John and I did with our children. Concordia and Colorado visits were all we could afford while living through medical school and surgical training. Neither John nor I had camped as kids. No way would any of our parents have gone camping. That was too much like the life their parents and grandparents had struggled to get out of. It was our generation who decided camping could be a leisure activity. The anthropologists call that *atavism*—

when an activity is no longer necessary for survival it becomes a sport, like hunting or paddling a canoe.

Our first neighbors in Pueblo had really gotten into camping. Their children bragged to our children about how much fun they had camping in the mountains, how many miles they hiked, how many fish they caught. John, who never passed up a challenge, particularly one as simple as going camping, consented to our first foray into the wilds of Cripple Creek, on the ranch that belonged to my dad.

We went alone, not with the neighbors, who might make us feel foolish because we didn't know from borscht about pitching tents or setting up a campsite. The closest John had been was in the army in Korea where everyone—military or civilian—seemed to be camping. My experience had been limited to one-night stands with the Girl Scouts out at Twin Mounds in Kansas.

We packed up everything lying around loose and headed for the hills, dog and all. Up on a hillside out of sight of the house we chose Camp Weaver and tried to discourage curious cows intent on discovering the purpose of our invasion. With more than a little trouble John and the boys, ages four and seven, strung up a canvas lean-to between trees. That came in handy later as we crouched under its shelter during the hour or so of an ice storm. The children had pup tents, but crawling in during the middle of the day was frightening so we cowered under the tarp.

Our little dog, Digger, loved the cattle. As far as we knew, Digger had never been that close to such a big animal. Allison held him, comforting, since every time she let go Digger would race after more cows, chasing them ever closer to the house. John and the children tried to explain to the dog about the evils of chasing Grampy's cows. I just grabbed a rope and tied the little pest to a scrub oak near our camp. He raced frantically around the bramble until he wound himself down to the last few inches of tether then proceeded to try to choke himself to get even with me. We put him in the car, the only comfortable place on the ranch.

Somehow during the rain of ice all of our supplies had been drenched. Nothing beats soggy paper towels on a camping trip, particularly the maiden voyage. We huddled in the cold, cooking up some sort of a stew that bore slight resemblance to my carefully planned menu. Roasting the marshmallows almost saved the evening before we all bedded down in the darkest of dark night, listening to the cows foraging around our heads.

By five o'clock the next morning we were unloading the camping equipment out in the driveway and were headed for our own beds.

During the next years we honed our camping skills enough to enjoy many excursions with the Adams and the Curry families to such great places as Maroon Bells near Aspen and Bandelier Monument in New Mexico. All of us enjoyed those days.

Matt had been born by the time we really got into camping, a week at a time or so. He and Steve Curry, the same age, learned to walk in our campsite at the Sand Dunes in Colorado's San Luis Valley. For their faltering steps that firm sand proved hard enough to walk on but soft enough to fall on.

Something of the pioneer in each of us surfaces on a camping trip. John, compulsive surgeon that he was, insisted upon keeping the camp in apple-pie order at all times. He worked at it. From the Koreans he had learned the trick of sprinkling water from a bucket on a dusty campsite, then sweeping with a leaf rake or a wide broom. This he called "retting up the camp." Hours on end he would ret up the camp while the rest of us stirred up the dust with every step. It gave him something to do, I suppose.

Once or twice on every camping trip some of us, or all of us, would hike. John and the other father-doctors trudged with the older children across old toll roads into the San Luis Valley. We worked our way arduously up the narrow, steep, deep-cut trails of the Ancient Ones at Tsankawi, a memorable experience, especially since Indians of yesteryear did not have Weaver paunches and John kept getting stuck along the way.

At the Sand Dunes, the children of the Weaver and Curry families enjoyed the spectacle of their fathers going off alone to explore a pioneer cemetery up the side of the mountain. The kids had had it with hiking. They stayed behind to play in the stream. Mary Curry and I watched the babies.

The fathers returned to camp in almost no time at all. John's face was the color of cranberry jelly. Vernell Curry seemed about to pass out. Inside our tent, John threw himself on the cot, gasping.

"That Vernell Curry is the fastest [expletive deleted] walker I have ever seen!" I went to get him some water.

Over in the Curry's tent, Vernell Curry, pediatrician extraordinaire, flung himself on his cot.

"Mary," he croaked, "John Weaver walks faster than any man I have ever known!"

That camping excursion ended our family career but not because those two had nearly raced each other into heart failure. This was Labor Day weekend—a famous Labor Day weekend when Colorado had snow earlier than ever recorded before. Mothers and kids snuggled in the cars or crowded around the hot-air hand dryers in the ladies' room while the fathers and big boys struggled to fold tents covered with wet sand and snow.

On the long drive back to Pueblo, John voiced loudly his considered opinion:

"The reason most people camp is it makes your vacation seem twice as long."

We Weavers never camped again.

7
NOW, ABOUT THOSE GRANDPARENTS . . .

J oe, let's go feed the chickens." With those words, Allison wrapped her Grandfather Weaver around her little finger.

The Weavers kept chickens in their back yard in Concordia, to the delight of our youngsters but the dismay of neighbors sick of crowing roosters. From the time they moved to Republican Street in 1924 Joe and Vesta had kept chickens in town. Vesta had the laying hens. Joe raised game cocks. Don't get me wrong, here, Joe Weaver did not raise fighting chickens; he and Vesta just liked the spectacular plumage of the game cocks and treated them as pets.

One of the big events for little Weavers, ours and their cousins, would be the day Joe brought Hector, King of the Roosters, into the kitchen and held Hector erect on the kitchen scale while Vesta took a picture of the two of them posing for posterity. Knowing Hector's weight from month to month apparently meant a lot. For these photography sessions, Joe needed heavy gloves. Hector objected strenuously to his weigh-ins, squawking and pecking in all directions, which delighted the children even more.

Joe also posed with his home-grown tomatoes on that scale every summer. It didn't take long for the little people of the family to understand that Joe's chickens and his tomatoes were the key to enjoying that wonderful back yard.

Actually, Joe Weaver had a hard time disguising his disappointment when his first grandchild turned out to be a girl, but Allison won him over all by herself as soon as she learned to say "Joe."

Joe had been an athlete, a runner at Kansas University. My sons still have some of Joe's medals from the KU Relays. When I first knew him in the early '40s he was still in pretty good shape, about 5′11″, weighed 175, I'd guess. Later on, his penchant for making and sampling home brew put more of a paunch on him, but Joe never could have been called a big man—not like his sons or like Vesta's family. He kept his curly hair in a crew cut and always wore bow ties. (Now, what made me remember the bow ties after all these years?) Joe Weaver could have been described in many ways, I suppose, but nobody ever referred to him as a "snappy dresser."

Joe had devoted most of his active parenting life to making a fine athlete of his son, John. John's older brother, Joe, Jr., had no interest or ability on the football field or in the swimming pool, but John was a natural and Joe made the most of that. Hour after hour, day after day, year after year, Joe coached John to be a champion swimmer even though the Concordia High School had no swim team and no coach.

When he was not holding the stop watch beside the school pool, Joe sat in the bleachers during every football practice and certainly never missed a game. He never missed telling John how to do it better, either.

Concordia won the League, John won the honors, then John set state records for breast stroke and back stroke which "stood" for many years in the annals of Kansas high-school swimming and the local AAU, for which Joe gave himself full credit. Joe considered himself a man's man.

༄

During this lifetime I've met some conservative people, but when it comes to outright compulsion for security, Joe Weaver takes the cake. This angle to his personality figured into his grandparenting, so it counts here. Perhaps his negativity stemmed from what we now recognize as mild depression. At any rate, Joe's father and his two older brothers were doctors. Doctor Asa Weaver had his own hospital and a lively practice in Concordia. Brother Ross Weaver practiced radiology at St. Joseph Hospital there. Glenn Weaver lived in west Texas, I believe, where he was a psychiatrist.

The last thing Joe wanted was an M.D. after his name, even

though the family expected that. The tension and constant pressure of KU medical school drove him absolutely crazy. He agonized over every pop quiz and suffered through every lab report. The thought of being responsible for the well-being of patients was more than he could bear.

When Asa Weaver, M.D., died during Joe's second year of medical school, that poor miserable soul beat it home to Concordia as fast as he could get there, settled on a farm the family owned out east of town, married Vesta, and never again thought of being a doctor.

Even the insecurity of farming worked on Joe with his negative attitudes. He hated it when it rained, worried even more when it didn't. Vesta and the rest of the family understood this, so everyone sighed with relief when Joe Weaver went to work for the Post Office.

It is significant to note here that Glenn Weaver, the shrink, brought his wife and young son to live with Joe and Vesta during the Depression when postal clerks were paid but doctors were not. Joe pointed that out regularly.

Being a postal clerk in the days when sorting mail by hand involved knowing every route of every train west of any given point suited Joe. He worked hard at being the best sorter and the most efficient clerk at the window on sunny or cloudy days, with a regular paycheck and Vesta to drive him back and forth to work. He worked 7:00 to 3:00 so he had after-school time for coaching John and, years later, spending time every day with the grandkids when we spent half-summers in Kansas during medical school.

His talent for anticipating the worst of any situation never left Joe. Our youngest son, Matthew, was born when Allison was thirteen, her brothers eight and eleven. All three of the "big kids" absolutely adored their new brother and cared for the baby devotedly.

Joe, whose favorite expression about any child was "poor little soul," would watch this carrying-on about baby Matthew and shake his head sadly.

"It's a shame those bigger kids are so crazy about Matt," he'd say. "If anything happens to that baby and he gets sick and dies, those kids won't be able to take it."

Typical Joe Weaver logic.

Happily, Joe was not around when Matt broke his head. One morning I asked eight-year-old Ross to watch his baby brother, who was lying on the couch. I went to the kitchen for some reason and Matt rolled off, hitting his head on the foot of the coffee table. That poor little head had a dent like an old ping pong ball, so off we went to the doctor, the hospital, surgery, and all the rest. Our darling baby boy came out a cue ball kid. Joe would have wound up on the couch himself.

Months later I realized Ross spent time out in the back yard alone, after dark in that big yard by himself. One evening I questioned him.

"Ross, what are you doing out there in the back yard in the dark all by yourself? It's cold. What's the idea?"

Ross gave me a soft smile. "Mother, I didn't want you to know this, but I've been going to the back yard to pray."

Pray? An eight-year-old meditating in the garden, as they say?

"How lovely, Ross." I smiled at him. "Are you praying about anything in particular?" Christmas was coming.

Again this sappy smile. "Mother, I've been praying to God to forgive me because I let my baby brother fall off the couch and hurt his head so he had to have an operation."

"How thoughtful of you, Ross. You are such a fine big brother," I said as I reached to hug him.

Ross reeked of cigar smoke.

"While you've been praying have you been smoking your dad's cigars out there in the dark by yourself?"

"Oh, no."

"Ross, you smell like cigar smoke. Are you telling me you haven't been smoking?"

"Mother, I have not been smoking. I have been trying to smoke but I can't get 'em lit. So I just tried. I did not smoke."

That story might be beside the point, but it has always been a favorite of mine. Ross is not too fond of my telling it.

❧

I have quizzed my sons and daughter about their memories of their grandparents. Of Joe they have agreed. They recall the rides. Joe and Vesta would pile grandkids into their Ford and take off across country roads for hours, stopping in farming communities along the way for pop or ice cream.

Vesta did the town driving, Joe took the wheel when they headed for the country, but both drove that old Ford as if it had an automatic shift. Once down the alley and onto Republican Street, they shoved that old car into second and never touched the gearshift again until they needed to back up. Cloud County, Kansas, is hilly, green and pleasant along the Republican River. The children collected limestone fossils and Vesta took pictures of kids lined up in front of windmills.

When they grew old enough to visit grandparents by themselves Joe loved taking our boys to his barber. They returned from visits to Kansas with crew cuts that were generally very bad, but they had had a good time with Joe.

One favorite place to visit on their rides was the ramshackle house of Boston Corbett, Concordia's celebrity. Boston Corbett's claim to fame was shooting John Wilkes Booth, after which he (Corbett) was dishonorably discharged and moved to Kansas.

They also explored the country around Glasco, Kansas, where Vesta had grown up. Joe made fun of Vesta, constantly teasing about Glasco, Kansas, in the heart of the Solomon Valley where it's richest and widest and best. Just like some of the small town "humor" we had down around McPherson.

The Weavers lived across the street from the high school, just up the hill from the athletic field. Their yellow frame house with a great front porch typified mid-America without any of the frills or "pretensions" of some of Concordia's wealthier neighborhoods.

Vesta cooked on her old gas stove long after similar models were appearing in museums and antique stores. That seemed to be Vesta's choice. Vesta Cool Weaver made a fetish of not "putting on airs." Taller than Joe by an inch or so, Vesta out-weighed her husband by ten pounds most of her life. She was a sturdy, stocky, sensible woman who wore heavy black oxfords and braided her hair. Her clothes reflected her disdain for any fanciness: one black dress for funerals and church, housedresses, which she usually trimmed with a bit of rick-rack and a front zipper. She knew everyone in town and was universally admired for her kindness and caring for others. Not that Vesta was a saint. She simply cared.

Mostly, however, Vesta cared for Joe. This irritated me early in our marriage. "She lets Joe walk all over her," I'd say. "She waits on him hand and foot, fixing him special salads, driving him to work, shushing the kids so Joe can rest, running all of his errands, putting up the storm windows. She even peels tomatoes for him. She's nuts!" I yelled at John.

He'd always defend her taking all this guff and his reasoning made some sense: Vesta'a mother had died when Vesta and her brother and sister were quite small. They had grown up in a house with their father and their maternal grandmother, so Vesta had no role model of wife-type behavior to follow. She had no real example of marriage, so she assumed Joe was generally right about most everything. She probably thought all wives were indentured to their spouses.

After two years of college, she had married Joe. After a year or so they settled into their idea of marriage: Joe worked at the post office and Vesta worked at everything else. She emphasized simplicity, pragmatism and common sense with the rest of us.

Our memorable meals at Weavers, for Vesta was an excellent cook, invariably are recalled as the times Vesta made hamburgers. Vesta's gravy, pies, fried chicken (fresh from the back yard) and delicious biscuits could not hold a candle to her hamburgers. She cooked and served only four at a time, even for the entire family. Not fat, bulky burgers but skinny burgers in skinny buns. Hot from her stove, each patted fresh and instantly fried. For years I tried to duplicate the magic of Vesta's hamburgers, but never made the grade.

Vesta's cooking far outshone her housekeeping. Her favorite expression, "a man on a galloping horse would never see it," applied to any sort of flaw or oversight in their home. If some more important project like a ride to the country interfered, almost any sort of household chores could wait.

⌒

It is important to note here, however, that Joe and Vesta were savers. We'll go into that later, but for now picture a back-porch work bench piled high with old newspapers, rusted tools, jars of nails, skillets without handles and baskets full of holes. The buffet in the dining room could be seen in its original glory only when a death in the family brought everyone to the Weavers and Vesta cleared off the buffet for the company. The walls were covered with pictures of everyone they had ever known because "Joe likes things out where he can see 'em."

I asked Allison, now over forty years old, how she remembers Vesta. Allison's eyes mist when the name is mentioned.

"Vesta could always fix things. Vesta could always make everything all right. I knew when I was little I could depend on Vesta to help me. She made things for me—like that purple square-dance skirt and doll clothes. She sang in the car or whistled. Sometimes she'd just pat my hand."

The boys felt the same way. Whatever needed doing, Vesta could do it. They undoubtedly got that message from Joe. And generally they were right. Vesta could fix almost anything. Some of the extension cords draped around the dining room caused some of us to shudder, but Vesta made almost everything work.

Until John's graduation from medical school in Philadelphia, when my dad loaned his new station wagon to the Weavers to drive east for the big event and help us move our meager belongings westward, Vesta had never been out of Kansas. Her father, a most successful farmer and banker, had taken his son to market in Kansas City, but his girls stayed right on the farm where he knew they belonged. He also left his farm to the men of the family, not the women. Typical of the attitudes of the day, I'd assume, but outrageous by today's standards.

In spite of her truly provincial upbringing and her incomplete college education, Vesta Weaver had one of the keenest minds I have ever known. Her inquisitiveness, her interest in the world around her, her obsession with words and their derivation, made her good company from the first day we met. These qualities she imparted to her grandchildren. Vesta seldom left a question unanswered. She and the kids would look it up, whether something from conversation or a book or a Scrabble game. The more I write about her, the more I realize how much I admired Vesta. We were good friends.

∽

My own parents resembled the Weavers only in being Kansans. Joe and my father could not have been more different. Joe was friendly enough, certainly, but John Allison greeted everyone he met as a long-lost buddy, telling funny stories or making comic observations to the delight of anyone around. Dad also lived by taking risks, by inventing and promoting all sorts of schemes, which sometimes worked but which sometimes went right back to the drawing board or into the trash.

Some said John Allison and John Weaver looked enough alike to be father and son. I never agreed, but the two of them did have a lot in common and enjoyed throughout their lives a special bond. Both weighed well over two hundred pounds on a yo-yo sliding scale. Both were barrel-chested and had slim hips so their trousers were always at half mast. Dad had wavy thick hair that had been red in his youth. John was more of a blonde. They died less than three years apart, and both left all of us with some very funny and some rather painful stories. But that had little to do with the grandparent part that concerns our children and my parents at this point.

The lifestyle of my parents contrasted with that of John's folks from the beginning. My folks were always traveling, and business kept my father on the road when Mother was at home. The money was different, certainly, and that made one of the big contrasts in their grandparenting.

Basically, John's parents "did" for our children while my parents "bought" for them. That meant a lot for us as parents to appreciate on both sides. Our children's winter coats and other major wardrobe items were paid for by my mother while John trained for surgery at resident's starvation wages. Once in a while my dad would drop off an extra car for us to use, or they would offer us "extra" furniture, or Dad brought John some of his expensive clothes he claimed he'd tired of wearing. My parents paid for my cleaning help in Kansas City.

CO

Looking back, I am relatively certain there were chickens at my folks's house, too, but they lived on a splendid ranch north of Colorado Springs where the gardener tended the tomatoes and the farmer's wife brought in the eggs. Nobody weighed the roosters in the kitchen like Joe did in Concordia. Foothill Farms certainly did not resemble Republican Street in any way. There were ponies, a swimming pool, lakes stocked with trout and teeming with bluegills, a guest house, and a big house filled with treasures not to be touched by little hands. All with Pikes Peak as a backdrop.

Allison and Chris were the first grandchildren on either side of the family. They paved the way for the rest of the grandchildren, including two more of our own. Ross was born in Kansas City, Matthew after we moved to Colorado.

Moving to Colorado brought much closer extended-family contacts, since by that time all of my sisters and my parents lived in Pueblo and Colorado Springs. The Colorado grandparents who occasionally had been a part of our children's lives now lived just up the road. Joe and Vesta Weaver were farther away than ever, therefore more fun to visit for longer vacations without John and me.

My mother, Marn Allison, turned out to be an entirely different kind of a grandmother than Vesta or my own Grandmother Allison. She is, after all, an entirely different kind of a person. Her primary concern has been orderliness. My mother keeps things neat. She prefers her environment quiet and her surroundings undisturbed. That means our children have probably driven her to distraction and her responses have been predictable: She has enjoyed her grandchildren less because they annoyed her just by being kids. To say that this has resulted in stress on both sides would be the understatement of the year.

I feel safe in saying that my mother's greatest joy as a grandmother came from being with "the little girls." Our youngest sister Mary and her family lived on the ranch with Mother and Dad when their three daughters were little girls. They were three of the prettiest, cutest, brightest youngsters I have known, and Mother truly enjoyed having them around. The little girls traveled with Grammy and Grampy. The little girls were model grandkids.

Most of all, the little girls were not little boys.

Two stories about my son Chris come to mind. Just able to walk around and explore at Grammy's house, Chris headed for the forbidden coffee table and lifted the lid of an antique glass butter dish, one of Grammy's Things. Mother yelled at him, "put that down, Chris!" so startling him that he slammed the lid back on, smashing it into a thousand pieces and breaking both his and Grammy's hearts.

Chris's heart was certainly not broken years later when we took Mother with us to watch Chris in his first football game. The bleachers were small, right behind the bench. Mother watched Chris going in and out of the game as long as she could stand it. Then she called shrilly, "Chris! Chris! Pull up your socks, honey!" The look on that 16-year-old tackle's face broke my heart.

We need to remember that my mother apparently had never had much of a relationship with her own grandparents, therefore no role model or pattern to follow. Her own mother died before we girls spent time in that household. So Mother never saw her own mother as a grandmother.

Where do grandmothers come from? From the beginnings of our lives, that's where.

Besides that, during our growing up years Mother had to be the stabilizing influence, the Rock of Gibraltar, while her husband dashed around the country in one business venture and then another. We girls must have been four burdens to Mom, who has never been an extrovert in any sense of the word. She guarded us with her life. Dad turned out to be a great provider, but it was Mother who kept the family and the finances on an even keel. When grandchildren came along, Mother did the best she could in providing for our needs as mothers, but sitting on the floor playing cars with little boys simply was not her cup of tea. It has taken most of our family a long, long time to figure that one out.

Now she needs us as she never expected to, and the indignity of such dependence makes life even harder for all of us. Many families face such trauma these days. We just need to cope with aged grandmothers as we wished they would cater to our children. It's a matter of taking turns. Many grandmothers feel like my mother has felt for all these years. We expect Granny to gush over the kids like Ma Perkins over Effie, and that just doesn't happen sometimes.

Once more, in thinking out this book, I have asked opinions and recollections from my children. When I asked Allison what comes to her mind when I say Grammy, she did not hesitate. "To me, Grammy always looked unhappy. She never seemed to be having a good time while we were around."

❧

Dad, who had had no brothers and no sons, loved to gather together his grandsons for an excursion of his own planning.

On one occasion seven boys under twelve, I think, boarded the train at Pueblo with Grampy for a stay at Glenwood Springs, where they swam in the enormous hot-springs pool and ran wild all over the big hotel.

Even better, a couple of years later (before any of them could drive) the seven of them had The Trip with Grampy in one of the first Dodge motor homes. Only Matthew missed these vacations, being too young to go along. No girls, of course. They were invited to Laguna Beach or on a cruise ship.

In the motor home, Dad and his vagabonds traveled to Glen Canyon Dam and Lake Powell for a day or two on a houseboat, thence to Mexico, and a necessary (for Grampy) swing by Las Vegas. Years later, we are still learning about that journey, which must have lasted two weeks or more. After the first night in the van Dad chose to park at a motel every night where the boys could swim and their grandfather could sleep in the comfort of a real bed.

Our father always did have a tendency to overstock on groceries. He had that vehicle loaded to the hilt with institution-size cans of peaches, pork and beans, and all the rest. Some time during the second day on the road, Dad rounded a corner fast enough that an open number 10 can of peaches in syrup spilled out of the cupboards and covered the interior with sticky stuff. By the time they returned to Pueblo at least ten layers of extraneous material, from bread crusts to fish bait, had adhered to that original goo. We mothers hosed out the motor home while the boys sorted out their socks and T-shirts, absolutely ecstatic about the wonderful time they had had with their great old Grandad.

For three or maybe four summers we sisters and two cousins had a family camp up near Cripple Creek in Colorado. This, again, was a plan of my father's. He had bought property for summer pasture that had been a dude ranch. The sign at the gate read, "Modern Cabins." Mothers and children spent a month or more each summer while the fathers (who were in-laws, after all) came up on weekends.

We appreciated Dad's plan. We ran pretty much on a schedule and on the unspoken agreement that we would discipline only our own children. Expenses we shared on a complex "people-day" basis. Our adventures included bears tipping over the garbage can and one small girl eating insect-repellent tablets. We hiked and fished a little, ate a lot, and enjoyed each other's company until our children wanted

to stay at home for swim teams and other activities more interesting to them.

This Cripple Creek project has taken on a different slant since my children have grown up enough to discuss growing up with me. Sometimes that takes quite a while. Looking back, I am not sure whether we dragged the kids and the dogs and the groceries and the linens and the cleaning supplies and the insect spray up there to provide a special environment for them or to please my dad, whose big idea the whole thing had been. I do know my "good times" up there taught me to ask, rather than to direct, the activities of my family when I have taken time to consider my motives.

John was aware of this negative effect of planning for the family. "Let's not have any command performances with our kids," he often said. Case in point: Long after widowhood hit me I hung on to a charming log house in the mountains, thinking my kids and their families could spend time there. Such was not the case. Eventually I sold the house and split the money, a much more reasonable solution, it turns out. But that concerns parenting more than grandparenting.

✌

First of these four grandparents to die was Vesta. That was not at all in accordance with Joe's plan. He had preached and "jawed at" Vesta for all the years I had known them about exactly what she should do when he died (kill the old dog and get a new car). He never considered surviving beyond her; Weaver men just didn't do that. Cancer cancelled Joe's plans and reinforced my belief in the sterling qualities of my mother-in-law.

"They say one person in four will die of cancer," she told me. "I don't know why I wouldn't be one of them. Old Doctor Kiene used to say back in the '30s that we've learned to cure so many diseases sooner or later everyone will die of either cancer or heart failure. I believed him. He was right."

Her pragmatic attitudes about dying matched or even exceeded her acceptance of life as it came to her. Not so with Joe, of course.

"Joe can't say the word 'cancer.' He can't talk about any of this," she whispered to me not long after her surgery. He never could.

As soon as the doctors in Concordia operated Vesta for cancer of the colon and found her case beyond hope, Vesta went to work preparing Joe for life without her.

Nobody who knew her will ever forget this, the toughest part of her life. Joe had been totally dependent on Vesta. He had never been to the supermarket, could not find his handkerchiefs or clean socks.

Vesta helped him make grocery lists, showed him how to pay the gas bill, wrote down the name and number of their plumber. She pointed out the pitfalls of buying cheap toilet paper and explained how to make the coffee. She demonstrated how to iron his shirts. When she could barely stand, she changed the sheets while he watched, stacked the dishes in the rack to dry.

As the disease brought on weakness and pain, she refused to go to the hospital.

"I'll stay right here with Joe," she told me. "He'll need me here with him."

She told her sister Grace how to braid her hair and where to find her black dress. Then, with her Episcopal priest half-way through the Lord's Prayer at her bedside, Vesta died. Just as pragmatically as she had lived.

Joe lasted almost ten years after Vesta. He had a relatively easy life for himself—walked his dog and went to football practice in good weather. He came to Colorado several times but refused to move away from Concordia. That was just as well. For a brief period, a distant cousin lived with Joe, but they were both too set in their ways to make much of a go of such an arrangement. After a few months, Katherine beat a hasty retreat to Seattle.

Joe did have a housekeeper, which worked better. Joe developed an aneurism of the aorta for which he refused corrective surgery on the advice of his son the surgeon.

"You don't want that, Joe. You've outlived all the rest of your family already. Why risk being an invalid when you're nearly 80?"

On Thanksgiving Day 15 years ago, I stood at the foot of Joe's bed in good old St Joseph Hospital.

He opened his eyes, smiled, said, "Thanks for everything, Frances."

I replied, "Well, thank you, Joe."

He closed his eyes and died, at peace, with nothing more to worry about.

Nothing more for him to worry about. For John, the pain had only started.

I mentioned earlier about the saving habits of the Weavers. Much as I admired Vesta, she still hung onto too much stuff. Both of them did. Newspapers stacked in piles, but more than that. There were closets filled with useless junk that could have been disposed of years ago instead of leaving it all for John to have to clear away after his brother, his mother and his father had died.

John Weaver was a bright, sensitive, pragmatic surgeon. He was also a caring member of his own family who should not have been forced to relive his entire life clearing out dusty Hallowe'en costumes, tattered football practice jerseys, nine million framed portraits of people so long dead he wouldn't have recognized their names if anyone had bothered to label them. Any one of us can be more thoughtful of our own children and grandchildren by leaving this world in a more or less orderly fashion.

All of those baby blankets, high school annuals, photo albums, and calendars from the Fidelity State Bank could have been trashed in the '40s. The broken toy trucks and the air rifles had outlived their usefulness but they still brought tears and pain to the family member who relived childhood alone in those dusty, box-filled closets.

Oh, John's brother's children were there, and maybe his widow; I don't remember. The point is, almost all of this accumulation of trivial trash predated our lives together. I could share neither his reminiscences nor his remorse. I had no idea why a grown man would cry over a Buddy-L truck or come to pieces over the rusted remains of a minimal Lionel train set.

More than once John had offered to help his father clear out the debris in the house while he was still healthy, but Joe had always laughed.

"No. That's what you get to do, Johnny. Ha, ha, ha."

There'll be no such last laughs at my house, believe me. I'd like to think anyone smart enough to be reading this book will be too smart to pull such a mean trick on his offspring, but you never know. As for myself, I would far rather ask both succeeding generations frequently, "do any of you want any of this?" and clear the decks for my own peace of mind and their future serenity.

You'd be amazed how little I have to dust these days. We can joke about it, but this business of "clearing out" after the death of the old folks is as much our responsibilty as our offsprings'. Not being pessimistic, just practical.

Planning for the future of his future generations occupied much of my dad's thinking. Mostly he set up financial matters for my mother and for the bulk of his estate to go to his grandchildren. Skip generation, I think he called it. He also left his affairs in the hands of friendly bankers, with Mother already moved out of the family home into the condo-town house frame of mind, which made it easier for all of us when his heart gave out after hip surgery in 1977. By that time he had three great grandchildren and he left behind thirteen grandkids who loved laughing and joking with Grampy.

All in all, the words most used by his second generation offspring to descibe my dad include "generous," "funny," "kind," and "successful." Almost all of his grandchildren now adult marvel at the way that man could make money and enjoy life at the same time. That leaves a goal to shoot for, too. A respectable heritage from all sides.

♣

LET'S GET THESE PEOPLE STRAIGHT!

In these next chapters I'll be mentioning children and grand-children with wild abandon. You can't know the players without a program, so here is my version of a family tree as affects this book.

JOHN WEAVER, M.D.		FRANCES ALLISON WEAVER	
ALLISON	CHRIS	ROSS	MATT
*m.*Roger Swift	*m.*Mary	*m.*Judy	*m.*Sherry
Whitney Swift	*Donald*	*Jason*	*Chigger*
	Andrew	*Sarah*	*Nikki*
	Jennifer		

Jason claims the right to first-born, although he is not the oldest. Donald, Andrew, Jennifer, Chigger and Nikki all came into our family by marriage after Jason and Whitney were born. Miss Sarah is youngest, having arrived at the very end of 1976. John was a part of the lives of all of these kids except Chigger and Nikki, since Matt and Sherry were married three years after John died.

Chris adopted Mary's three children, all of whom are older than Jason and Whit. Therefore Don, Andy and Jenny are Weavers. Sherry's two girls are now married, living in California, with new last names of their own.

More about all of this in chapter 9.

♣

8
WHAT KIND OF A GRANDMOTHER ARE YOU?

What child ever attracts more attention than the first-born grandchild? Jason Weaver entered our lives while his father, our son Ross, served in the Viet Nam theatre with the Marines and his beautiful young red-haired mother lived at our house in Pueblo. John and I got into grandparenting full speed ahead.

Most grandmothers in their 40s wait until the first kid is toddling before deciding on a grandmother name. Let's talk about that. Before Allison's wedding in 1967 one of my best-friend neighbors, Mercy McIlroy, advised me wisely, "choose your own inlaw-grandma name right now. Don't leave anyone making up stupid nicknames or wondering what to call you. Name yourself and stick to it. You'll be doing everyone in the family a favor."

Mercy hit the nail on the head that time. I chose "Oma," naming myself after the German grandmother I admired who had been our neighbor in Philadelphia. Oma I have been for 24 years to in-laws, grandkids and the children's friends. Nobody else ever calls me that name and my gang never call me anything else. It's our signal of our own special relationship. I cannot tell you how much that can mean, or how much I thank Mercy for such simple, great advice. (Have I been clear? My own children call me Mother, their spouses call me Oma.)

John had a small snag in choosing his family name. We laughed ourselves silly, the entire family in a car before Allison's wedding, suggesting names for the patriarch of our little brood. Chris, high-school age, thought "Fatso" would do, but John objected: "Everybody else calls me that." He settled on "Jocko," which Allison and her young husband, Roger, accepted readily.

Shortly before Jason was born, John had the opportunity to do a big favor for Judy, Jason's mother. Judy, overcome, beamed at John.

"You're a real pal," she said and hugged her helpful father-in-law.

"Pal" became John's in-law name from that moment—except for Allison's family, who still refer to their Weaver grandfather as Jocko.

What I'm saying here bears paying attention to. We, as oldsters, establish a unique relationship with our growing families by special names for each individual. The Weavers insisted on being called by first names as a friendly, no-frills gesture. That choice was their own, but it bothered me a lot. Anyone in town could call John's dad "Joe." I think names are more important than that in our family shorthand language.

Two months after Jason's birth, our second grandson, Whitney Swift, was born in Illinois. Here again we consider names. None of these expectant parents consulted us about names for their babies. Judy and Ross chose Jason for their own reasons. Allison and Roger decided on Whitney totally unaware there had been an Uncle Whitney in my family. But then, I never cared much for Uncle Whitney anyway. Discussions of naming babies after relatives or heroes or friends can be tedious and non-productive. We never found out what little girls might have been named in those families until Sarah arrived six years later.

Whit and Jason are almost 21 now. Both are college juniors, both fine scholars and straight-arrow guys. From their baby days, we have enjoyed each other. Their christening together in Pueblo (Allison and Roger had brought Whit from Chicago, Ross had returned from the Marines) demonstrated for the first time how different these boys will always be, yet how compatible.

Whit tended to be one very active child, scooting all around, making noises and waving things in the air. Jason, those few months old, sat or lounged passively in the buggy or on the floor, watching Whitney gyrate around him. Jason's blue eyes expressed wonder. Whitney's snappy black eyes have always meant excitement.

When these boys were old enough to walk and talk, we all had a picnic in the Beulah Mountain Park near Pueblo. (By this time John and I had moved to our mountain home in Beulah.) Both little boys laughed and clapped as we pushed them in their swings. Then Jason tired and left his swing, walking right in front of Whit for a collision that flattened Jason and sent both toddlers into tears.

Later, Whit sidled up to his blonde cousin. "Want to swing some more?"

"No," Jason replied from his mother's lap. "I'm afraid you'll knock off my other ear."

We missed much of Whitney's growing up since they moved to Houston. John worried about that—having a grandson who would probably turn out to be a Texan. Apparently that was not a Weaver thing to do. John's fears surfaced when Whit tried to pry from his grandad the secret of what he'd get for Christmas. This happened at Thanksgiving time when Whitney neared three years old. Of course John refused to give away the secret of the gift.

"What letter does it start with?" Whit demanded.

"S," said John.

"Snikes?" pounced the excited little boy.

"Snikes? *Snikes?* Get that kid out of Texas!"

But stay in Texas he did, and the whole family. Whit and his parents are more Texan than Sam Houston or George Bush.

These boys and I have always loved kites. I am a real nut about

kites, no doubt, and four-year-old Whitney understood that (better than the rest of the family, I might add.)

One day in Houston, arriving at the Galleria to shop, Whit informed me about a kite store in this center that had nothing but great kites for sale. I expressed interest of course, but the grandfather in the front seat allowed as how both Whit and his grandmother had enough kites already.

For one fleeting moment Whitney seemed disappointed, then he brightened as he looked at the three of us, two grandparents and his mother. "I've got a great idea," said the kid. "Let's break up into smaller groups." We did.

About that same age, Jason spent quite a lot of time with Pal (John, remember?) and me in Beulah. We had great times hiking in the hills and picnicking. Jason's favorite place to eat lunch was the roof of our little barn, where he could perch along with kittens and munch on tuna sandwiches—shared, of course.

Jason helped with the cooking. He and I became adept at making our own potato chips, our specialty for a while. He also helped in serving the plates. Before dinner one evening he announced, "Oma, tonight I'm going to say 'yum' for my broccoli. Not 'yuk.'"

As I put the food on his plate he turned very serious. "Oma, I think I'll wait 'til next time to say 'yum' for my broccoli." He's a junior at Stanford, but I'm not sure his "yum for broccoli" day has arrived yet.

But his manner of expression has always been gentle. He must have picked up that trait from his mother. After a picnic in the mountains in the rain, with burned hot dogs and wet chips, Jason said it all:

"Oma, next time you say 'Jason, do you want to go on a picnic?' I hope I say no."

Most of all, Jason helped Pal. He loved carrying in firewood because he had his own stack of "Jason wood" the right size for Pal to load up his outstretched arms and stack sticks beside the big Pal logs. Jason fed the kittens, walked the dogs, and rode the horses; he picked the beans and peas from the garden and waded in the creek. We loved the snow with our sleds and visited with Beulah neighbors. His life visiting us was totally typical of the first grandchild, I'm certain of that.

One day Jason asked to have a party. That meant we'd "go out on the patio and sit and smoke and tell jokes." Jason carried along two

Crayolas, one to "smoke," one to use for a match. He crossed his legs in his huge chair, totally relaxed.

"Now tell me some little kid jokes," he instructed. I failed miserably to amuse him. He and I constituted the party. No other joke-tellers available.

Last gasp, I told him about the chicken crossing the road. Very funny. Jason surveyed the creek, the yard, the trees above. Then he puffed on his Crayola.

"Oma, do you know why the duck went across the bridge?"

"Why, Jason?"

"He wanted to be with your chicken."

So now you've heard enough cute-kid stories to know we Weavers have been blessed with brilliant, clever, remarkable grandchildren. You're lucky I don't carry pictures in my wallet or run into you at the supermarket to tell you the latest cutest sayings of those offspring. I'll spare you many more such tales, even about the time Whitney tried to convince me he could stay up until 9:30 because he was gifted.

We "broke in" on these two boys, then happily added Miss Sarah in Jason's family and acquired five more grandchildren by marriage. Two of my favorite people, the wives of sons Chris and Matt, had children from previous marriages. This pattern certainly is not unusual these days. Perhaps an entire book could be written about grandparenting an "added" family, but I'm going to devote the next chapter to the subject to explore the best I can from our experiences. For right now, I'll say families form in many ways, now. What's most important seems to me to be acceptance expressed in terms kids can understand.

I am forced to admit about the birth of Sarah Jensen Weaver, having a baby girl to snuggle and cuddle pleased me more than almost anything in my adult life. Little girls have a way of grinning just right, so grandparents melt. Yet Miss Sarah has been the same quiet, unflappable child her brother Jason had been, at least until she reached about four. Then some of her feminine temperament surfaced the day she refused to attend her own birthday party. By and large, however, Sarah occupies her own niche in the family.

She wasn't much more than four when this tiny blonde cherub overheard a conversation between her brother, her parents, and me about the relative importance of Christmas and Easter in the Christian year. None of us paid the slightest attention to the little girl at the end of the table.

Next day, Sarah cornered Jason and me to pursue the same subject. Jason must have been about eleven. He told Sarah that Christmas and Easter were equally important. Sarah was furious.

"Jason Weaver," she stomped, "Do you mean to tell me you don't love the Baby Jesus more than some dumb old rabbit?"

We need to be more thoughtful, or more aware, of children of that age, because they often think one step beyond us.

We all thought we had dealt with John's sudden death in an affirmative, reassuring way with all of the grandkids. We tried more than anything to help them face the fact of his dying in a positive way. But Sarah sort of got lost in the shuffle as far as I was concerned. She was much more understanding of the sense of crisis and grief than any of us knew.

I want other parents and grandparents to know this. Instead of thinking, "she's too little to comprehend," her parents and I should have done more with her. I'm not sure just what that could have been, but lately I've seen children's books on the subject, which I wished I had known about at the time.

Months after John died I took some of the grandchildren to the Beulah Cemetery at their request to see where he had been buried. The children had not attended the burial services because John had been cremated and their parents felt it would be too traumatic to see Pal reduced to a small bronze box. But Sarah went with us to see the burial site and the stone marking Pal's grave. Four-year-old eyes filled with disgust, Sarah turned to the rest of us.

"Is this where Pal is died?" We nodded. "Well," she said matter-of-factly, "It's no wonder. He can't get any air down there."

Obviously, we had missed somewhere.

More often than not, the loss of a grandparent or even a great grandparent will be the first experience of death in a child's life. It seems to me that grandparents can serve a unique function in the life of a youngster by paying special attention at such times and placing the positive emphasis on the continuity of family life and traditions in succeeding generations.

Grandparents' opportunities to function as a part of the family might not be the same as when we played "mother, may I?" on the front walk and sneaked ginger cookies from the jar on the shelf in the basement stairway, but this day and age of working couples as well as single parents certainly expands the role a grandparent can play.

Parents have less time for playing with families, in spite of great protestations of "quality time togther" and other such buzzwords. Grandparents have the opportunity to get to know these youngsters on a different, individual, level by taking time to fill in where parents cannot be. Time spent in a zoo, at a park, playing miniature golf, running errands, reading aloud, learning to play Nintendo (the old folks, that is) sorting family memorabilia, or exploring nearby "points of interest" bring generations closer together. We all know that, but sometimes we let the moments escape without making use of time.

I have no illusions that my grandchildren will spend hours raving about what a great time they have enjoyed with Oma, but I do feel we know each other better and appreciate each other more because of times we have shared.

If they only say, "Oma was sort of nuts, but she added to my life, anyway," that's good enough.

If, some day, some time, one of them says, "I remember that. I learned about that with Oma," who could want more of life?

Probably I wish that for myself because they already feel that way about Pal.

♣

9
STEP BY STEP: NIKKI AND THE GAY RIGHTS PARADE

Would you like to drive my car?" With the possible exception of "what (how much) do you want for Christmas?" this question gets the most attention from a teen-age grandchild.

The first of my grandchildren to be invited to drive along was Nikki (Nicole) Gowin, one gorgeous, bright, dark-eyed, blonde 16-year-old whose mother married my son Matthew. I drove to California for the writers' conference at Santa Barbara in my spiffy Chrysler convertible one summer. My sister Middy had made the trip west with me from Colorado. I needed a companion for the return trip and asked Nikki to fly to the coast and share driving home.

I did ask her mother first. That's the rule for every grandmother-grandchild outing in our family: Ask Mother first.

Our travel plans included time in San Francisco to pick up some excess baggage arriving on the *Royal Viking Sea*, left over from a cruise earlier in the year. Nikki and I stayed at the Sheraton near Fisherman's Wharf to be near the dock for picking up the stuff. We had a glorious time, although I refused to take her to the Hard Rock Cafe. I don't know why, except it hardly seemed logical to go there with your grandmother.

Nikki never lost her beautiful smile. Anything seemed to be okay with her, until she asked if we could go downtown to see the Gay Rights parade. Slowly, carefully, I explained to Nikki that San Francisco is not Pueblo, Colorado. It's a different sort of town.

"But I'd like to see it, Oma. I've never seen anything about Gay Rights. I've never even seen anyone who's gay, I guess."

I tried to stay abreast of the '80s. "Nikki, there's no reason to be critical of people who have different lifestyles," I started lamely. "The reason I don't want to get into the middle of that crowd downtown is the possibility of demonstrations or even riots. This issue causes a lot of problems. People act sort of crazy. I don't want to risk you getting hurt or trampled in a crowd just to satisfy your curiosity. I'm responsible for getting you back home in one piece."

Nikki did not hide her disappointment, even when I suggested we could ride the ferry to Sausalito for a fine time of browsing wonderful shops and having a great lunch right on the water.

Off we set, taking the cable car to the Ferry Terminal in the center of San Francisco. Just as we rounded the corner after getting off the cable car we heard the roar of motorcycles and the street was filled with the "dike bikers" leading the parade I had chosen to avoid.

There they all came. The crowds along the sidewalk surged out into the streets. Catcalls and all sorts of greetings strange to our innocent ears surrounded Nikki and me. Pushing and shoving, the spectators were moving to get into the act.

Nikki's eyes looked like saucers. "This isn't my scene, Oma. How do we get out of here?" And off we went to the ferry.

Later she did remark, "That scared me, Oma. Just remember, you got us there. I didn't." She liked Sausalito much better.

Nikki and I had a good trip. We drove across the salt flats in Utah under an astonishing moon so full the entire world glistened. Our drive through the mountains of the western slope of Colorado thrilled both of us. When we turned into her driveway in Pueblo, I felt we had become better acquainted. That pleased me very much.

&

More and more families are made up of parts of other families, we all know that. Single parents, mothers and fathers divorced and remarried, other interruptions of the "traditional" lifestyle have their effect on the role of grandparents, too, don't they?

We don't use the word "stepchildren" very much any more, but I read a comment about the term "step-" which appealed to me:

"I love my stepchildren, and we have a wonderful relationship . . . but they are not my children. The role of the stepparent is challenging enough without inviting trouble, so let's leave well enough alone and bear with a smile the honorary (and honorable) title of step."

Objectors to the term probably relate to fairy tales. Cinderella did have a helluva time; Hansel and Gretel didn't do much better. Stepparenting surely can be a challenge. Grandparents need to be aware of the rewards and hazards of such a composite family.

Not long after Chris and Mary were married, their three children attended John Neumann School in Pueblo. One beautiful spring day I accompanied the Indian Kitemaster, Dinesh Bahadur, to that school for a kite-flying demonstration. Everyone on the schoolgrounds had a wonderful time. Kids and nuns were flying great kites. Everyone shouted in absolute delight.

Now, Dinesh Bahadur must be about five feet tall. He wears traditional Indian "pajama" outfits and bejeweled shoes curled up at the toes. He creates quite a sensation since kites "magically" fly for him when nobody else can manage to get the big one off the ground. The Neumann School children were entranced.

Mary's oldest son, Don, called to me, calling me "Oma."

Said the kid next to him, "Do you know that woman?"

"Sure," said Don. "She's my new grandma."

"Well," snarled his friend, "Your new grandpa sure does wear funny shoes."

That made the day for most of us. Obviously I remember the scene. It was the first time I had been called a "new grandma." That shed a different light on my relationship with those youngsters: They had other grandparents. I'd better not forget that and try to be the hot-shot grammy in their lives. Eventually, five children came into our lives through marriage.

♥

Let's look first at Nikki and her sister Angelina, whom we have called "Chigger." Cute girls. Smart girls. Real achievers in school and in their friendships. During the years Sherry and these girls lived on their own they fended well for themselves and managed to take care of each other while Sherry worked to support them. They never lived close to grandparents and had little contact with their relatives. Certainly they must have resented Matt moving into their mother's life, taking her time and attention from them and trying to be a part of their world. No degree in psychology to figure that one out.

Neither could I logically expect these girls to have the same warmth of feeling for me that I felt with Jason, Whit and Sarah. I had not cuddled them as infants, had not nursed their skinned knees or shared Easter bunnies or kindergarten programs with them as they grew. I had not read Dr. Seuss or recited *Winnie the Pooh* with these kids. They had never depended on me to pick them up after school or to play miniature golf or "go fish." They were young teenagers with a family feeling and traditions of their own. For me to think I could be the same sort of character in their lives as with the others would have been unrealistic.

But we could be friends and I could help out. When college time came, I wanted to encourage these girls and helped out with tuition and book money. Now that they are married we enjoy getting together whenever it's possible, but—face it—they don't feel about me the way I felt about any grandparent. Women who try to be "real grandmothers" complain to me about this once in a while in referring to family expectations with new batches of children involved. I'm not much help.

As a matter of fact, Chigger and I had the best time we have had since Matt and Sherry were married (six or seven years ago) just last spring. Chigger, her husband, Peter, and their 14-month-old baby, Cassidy, joined me for supper in San Francisco. I might have said we went out to dinner, but we did not. Old age has its rewards in getting a little smarter, anyway. I thought about that restless toddler in a San Francisco restaurant and dialed room service.

With a fantastic view of the Bay Bridge and space enough for a large couch and coffee table in my room, no better place for a party with a baby could have been found in the Bay Area. We dined on an assortment of appetizers and pastas while Cassidy roamed to her heart's desire, stirring messes of mayonnaise in her Coke glass and feeding broken cookies to the rest of us. Jason had joined us from Stanford. We had a glorious time. My only regret was not having thought of such a party for the two generations that came before Cassidy.

Mary's three children were all in grade school when their mother and Chris were married. Again, I should not have envisioned being an honest-to-God grandmother. Any merging of families automatically means there have been some times of trauma for the youngsters. Life has not been smooth in spite of the efforts of their mothers to provide the home life on which children thrive. Perfection doesn't happen for those of us who manage to stay in the same marriage and keep the home fires burning. The road to our door has been paved with good intentions, but most children involved in second marriages have become at least skeptical about the role of the adults around them.

Again we often need to be reminded, these have not been our children since birth. Even though only six or eight years old, boys and girls have a sense of how things happen in their own families. They cannot be expected to conform to another family's "ways" immediately, if at all. Chris adopted Mary's three children soon after their marriage. Those kids and I have had some good times together. Now they are grown and living away from home but we share some good memories.

Both Don and Andy were absolutely crazy about John. They paid attention to Pal. They loved being with him, as did the other grandchildren. After John died and I moved to upstate New York to go to college, both Andy and Jenny visited me at Lake George and in New York City. Andy and I rode the ferry to the Statue of Liberty and took a Gray Line tour through Chinatown. We rented a motorboat on Lake George and Andy was the "skipper."

Jenny is a real sweetheart. She and Sarah and I vacationed over in western Colorado when Jenny was about fourteen, Sarah about six. Same Chrysler convertible, and we had a fine time. We sang with the radio, explored the cliff dwellings at Mesa Verde, rode horses at a dude ranch, and generally had fun. We wound up in Taos, New Mexico, where a little Indian kid at the pueblo scared Sarah out of her wits for wading in "his" stream, but Jenny comforted her little cousin and all ended well.

Back east, Jenny roamed the backwoods of Vermont with me searching for a furniture-maker. At Lake George she learned to play pool on rainy days and to run my boat when the sun finally shone. Jenny and I are special friends, I hope, although we will never feel like family. Her California grandmother is closer. That makes sense.

The most important consideration with any of the families of our children has to be keeping our noses out. Swallow all that good advice. I made the near-fatal mistake of trying to interfere in the workings of one of these sons' parent-child relationships, and came close to alienating the entire bunch permanently. Now that I have recognized the futility of my former ways, we do get along much better. This holds true particularly for those mothers and children who were already a family with their own family structure before anyone named any of them Weaver.

I have to remember that.

IO
I WAS HERE BEFORE WITH MY GRANDMOTHER

Jason offered to share his minimal knowledge of New York City with his Stanford teammates. After all, Stanford had made it to the Final Four of the NIT basketball tournament, and being in the Big Apple was part of the package. Most of the players hadn't spent time in the city. Where to go? What to see? How to get there?

Jason said he could sort of get around. "I was here several times with my grandmother," he explained.

So what could he find, lead his college friends to enjoy? F. A. O. Schwartz! The world's greatest toy store! What else do you learn from being in New York with your grandmother!

New York City certainly does not top my list of great vacation spots for grandparents and grandkids—nor for anyone else, for that matter—but some of the youngsters of the family and I have had some "quality time" there. Other places come to mind readily, like the museum at Cañon City, the pueblos at Taos, or the glorious shores of Lake George, New York.

I will be the first to concede that I have more time for the grandchildren since I have been a widow. That's not good or bad; that's just a fact of life. Women in my position (and there are more of us every day) do have opportunities for shared time that we might ignore or fail to recognize. To hang back for one reason or another cheats ourselves out of some fine times and many opportunities to add to the lives of these kids while expanding our own horizons in the process.

Sarah had not turned four when we first went to the Colorado State Fair together. The rest of the family left at home, Sarah and I looked at, sat on, bought, drank, ate and rode whatever our hearts desired at the fair that day. She seemed amazingly happy; I loved every minute.

Finally, I said, "Sarah, I think you and I are just the right ages to go to the fair together."

Sarah stared at me from under the brim of her new straw cowboy hat. "Of course we are, Oma," she announced. "That's because we don't fight."

"You're right, Sarah. We don't fight, do we?"

"No, we don't. That's because I'm too little and you're too old."

We got along on those terms for years. Still do, I'd say, especially the "old" part.

ᘓ

Whitney came by himself to visit when I was living alone up in Beulah. All of the Colorado cousins gathered so we could camp overnight in the "playground" on our mountain property. No parents, just Chris's kids, Ross's brood, Whitney and I. There really is no need for me to tell you how that went—like any other half-baked camping trip planned by a grandmother. We had our difficulties even though we were just over the rise from the house. We were far enough away to have to use the old outhouse.

At the turn of the century that property in Beulah had belonged to a childless couple who doted on helping with the orphans at the Sacred Heart Home. Tucked back in a small ravine along a dry creek bed was an astonishing playground and campsite. An old school-style merry-go-round, two teeter-totters, and a cracked concrete "swimming pool" remained of a once-glorious place for the children and the nuns to enjoy summer outings. I loved that place hidden in overgrown scrub oak and tall pine trees. It felt like another world, so it's no wonder I wanted to camp there with my grandchildren. I will always be sorry we didn't have that place when our first batch of offspring were growing up.

Centered in the "camp" was a huge barbecue built of bricks and stone. A not-too-stable-looking roof of corrugated iron sheltered the fireplace from the weather. Rickety cabinets from someone's old kitchen served to store picnic supplies. One very long, low picnic table reminded us of the dozens of small children who had shared this mountain retreat.

Originally, the pool had been filled from the springs up the draw. These springs had dried up or caved in or both. We filled the pool from the well up beyond the house. With all of those cracks in the concrete we filled it a lot. That water stayed cold in that tree-sheltered spot, but the kids and I played around in the pool anyway. The builder of this mini-wonderland had run an ingenious system of pipes from the springs to the pool through the firebed of the barbecue. Can you imagine such an arrangement? Keeping a fire in the barbecue oven supposedly heated the pool for the good sisters and their charges.

A couple of sheds, one housing an old generator to provide electric lighting in the early days, completed our complex. At that point I had no knowledge of the Great Camps of the Adirondacks, but this was ours. The youngsters and I dragged a couple of tents down and the boys put them up. The oldest, Don, must have been about fourteen. Andy and Whit and Jason all had camping experience by that time, so they pitched in to make the place "right." Jenny and Sarah and I brought half the kitchen down the path from the house over the hill. We still had a couple of horses who hung around watching the operation. Chigger and Nikki hadn't joined the family, yet.

The kids cooked our burgers or whatever. I seem to recall Whit doing most of the cooking. It was during this adventure that Whitney, our Texan, told me about his new-found skill in making deals. I asked him what sort of deals he could make.

"Well, Oma," he started to explain, "for instance, my folks and I were camping down in Texas and my mom wanted to wash her hair. She needed two buckets of water and asked me to get the water for her. The pump had a lot of bees around so I didn't really want to do that, but we made a deal."

"Okay," says the dutiful grandmother, "what sort of a deal?"

"I got the water and Mom washed her hair and I don't have to eat three-bean salad for the rest of my life."

Can't you just see a little old man shuffling along at a church supper saying, "Oh, no, I don't have to eat three-bean salad because my mother washed her hair"!

Anyway, that was one of our camp stories.

In the manner of overenthusiastic campers the world over, we ate supper as soon as the camp was set up, sat around our fire (in the barbecue pit) until dark, and slept fitfully until just before dawn when the boys cooked all the bacon and we were ready to call it quits about 7:30. We returned to the log house as though we had crossed the Wide Missouri. And I went back for the kitchen stuff later.

My time-sharing with the grandchildren, so far, reminds me of the old story about the dignitary visiting a small village in Mexico who was astonished to see a wall covered with painted targets. In the absolute center of each target was a perfect bull's-eye. Shot directly in the middle. The man admired this, then asked who had accomplished this feat.

"Sir," said the mayor, "Juan has done this."

"Bring Juan to me!" thundered the big shot.

Juan turned out to be an eight-year-old boy.

"You have done this?" asked the visitor.

"Sí."

"But how could you do this? Each a perfect bull's-eye?"

"First I shot a bunch of holes in the wall. Then I drew the circles around them. It was not difficult, Señor."

Generally, therein lies the story of my life, particularly my relationships with the grandchildren. So far, the plan seems to be working.

ↀ

Five or six years ago I had the bright idea of giving my family a vacation for Christmas rather than buying individual sweaters that didn't fit and toys they didn't want. Except for Allison and her family, who Christmas with their other grandparents, our tribe spent a few days between Christmas and New Year's in San Diego. I had realized by that time that our family could be big enough to qualify for group rates at hotels, particularly since a couple of cousins and one of my sisters joined our crowd. This arrangement worked out very well because we stayed in a centrally located hotel and could very easily break up into smaller groups.

It was an expensive experiment, but well worth while. Our hotel stood beside Seaport Village, which made it possible for us to walk to shops and so forth without expecting the entire gang to "muster." Some rented a car for Disneyland. Others concentrated on the zoo. We all gathered for dinner almost every day. Our one big outing was a whale watch on an old masted schooner. That highlighted the trip for me.

Now that the older kids are living away from home or in college (happy to be at home for Christmas) we have not tried that again. You will have to buy a lot more books before I can manage another one of those.

Meanwhile, less expensive, more imaginative pursuits have us involved. While writing a travel book I found it necessary to find out what other travel writers had done in the field. One marvelously attractive book called *Roadside Food* so extolled the virtues of cheeseburgers prepared on a grill in an old-fashioned diner that I suggested to Sarah we ought to have our own quest for a perfect cheeseburger. That has been fun, but Sarah has reached sweet 14 now. She doesn't eat such fatty foods.

We did, however, make a trip east of Pueblo to locate a diner featured in the book. It was closed. We also tried the burgers at the Broadmoor in Colorado Springs. Nothing wrong there. Most of the rest of our search I have carried on in odd places like Dutch Harbor, Alaska, or in Malta, where a cheeseburger includes a fried egg. Then I write reports back to Miss Sarah. Once in a while we still consider cheeseburger exploration, although the dietary habits of young women these days are a complete mystery to me.

☙

Speaking of food and Sarah, however, Sarah and my sister Ann's granddaughter, Kacie, spent a week with me on Lake George and in New York City one July. Sarah was ten, Kacie a year or two older. On a Saturday evening, driving up to that glorious lake, I remarked quite simply, "Tomorrow would have been my forty-second wedding anniversary if Pal had not died. That's a long time ago, isn't it? Forty-two years."

The girls were quiet.

Next I said, "I would really appreciate it if you two would rouse yourselves in time to go to church with me in the morning. You're both so pretty. I want to show you off to my Lake George friends."

The girls were quiet. The girls were still quiet when I tried to awaken them for church. Apparently they were unable to get up in time to go through all the ablutions necessary at that age. I mumbled something mean and stomped off to church by myself, probably saying something about ungrateful brats and surely not in love and charity with my neighbors as befits a good Episcopalian.

When I returned, I found a note on my door.

"Oma. Change your clothes and come to the dock."

To the dock? My inflatable 12-foot yacht was tied to a small dock in the "still bay" of Cannon Point. When I reached the top of the path to the dock area, the two girls waited for me, escorting me to the boat.

You should have seen the party they had prepared for my anniversary! My rubber Zodiac, draped with a bright swim towel, looked like Cleopatra's barge. They had placed pillows for my back. On the seat rested a fine tray of fruits served in orange peel cups, dainty sandwiches, chips and all sorts of other goodies. Sarah and Kacie carefully assisted my stepping into the boat so as not to upset the tray, then they proceeded to row me out to the center of the bay for our party.

I not only ate my share of the refreshments, I ate a lot of crow that morning.

ભ

When those two girls and I arrived in New York City (on Amtrak from Albany) we stayed in the apartment of a friend of mine in the east 60s. We, too, found F. A. O. Schwartz, of course, and we tried shopping at Bloomingdale's. This turned out to be a learning experience I hadn't expected. The clerks were pushy, the merchandise not much different from what they had just seen on the mall in Pueblo, Colorado. The glamour associated with Bloomie's disappeared in an instant.

We did, however, experience much of the city. The Circle Line cruise always makes a good beginning, to set the scene of Manhattan Island. After that, we headed to Fifth Avenue and the girls became adept at hailing cabs, dodging traffic, and inspecting the wares for sale on the street corners. We took in a Broadway matinee, a musical—perhaps *Me and My Girl.* At the top of the Empire State Building Sarah and Kacie bought "medals" made of smashed pennies for all of their friends back home. You can't get those in Pueblo!

All in all, we had three good days in the city. The kids liked the hansom cab around the park, showed more than minimal interest in the Metropolitan Museum of Art, thoroughly enjoyed the mimes and other performers on the steps of the museum.

Speaking of the steps of museums, particularly in New York City, Jason and Whit and I had a tale to tell about that from the days when those boys must have been twelve or thirteen. The steps this time were those oft-photographed steps of the majestic judicial building on Wall Street where George Washington took his first oath of office as our president. Jason and Whit and I sat on those steps to eat a hot dog.

The boys chose to visit the New York Stock Exchange. Down on Wall Street we watched the frantic carrying-on of daily trading from the balcony provided for observers. That was as much an education for me as it was for my grandsons. Out on the street again, we wandered over to that majestic historical building with the Corinthian columns. Even grander than the court house in Pueblo, they decided.

The Museum of Modern Art had an exhibit inside the building. We couldn't miss that. As we wandered around gazing at some really far-out examples of today's modern art, Whit became more and more agitated.

"Oma, this stuff is just trash." In his Texas drawl it came out *trishe.* "Look at this," he'd rave. "Any kid in our fourth grade could have done better than that. And *that*—those don't look like children. They might as well be pictures of apes." That assessment reminded me of nothing more than the "emperor's new clothes" story and the impression has stuck with me.

చు

I want to get back to the first of this chapter before we leave the subject of New York City.

Jason's presence in the city with the Stanford team had a special meaning for the two of us. One of our finest summer excursions had been before he began his senior year in high school in Pueblo. Jason can qualify as an outstanding kid on anyone's roster. Some days I fear some couple will appear out of nowhere claiming Jason is really their kid, mixed up in the hospital nursery. Together with his sister Sarah and his cousin Whitney, Jason performs well as a student, an athlete and a leader in his school situations.

That summer—1988, as I recall—Jason had been hounded by basketball coaches all over the country trying to recruit him for their teams. I spent most of that summer back east. NCAA rules prohibit person-to-person recruitment or interviews except when the student visits the campus on his own, or some such regulation. At any rate, it seemed to me the boy needed to look at these campuses and get a feeling for these universities before making a commitment. His parents agreed. So Jason and I had our own college tour. This turned out not only to be great joy for me, and a help for him, but also of value to his parents, since Ross and Judy certainly could not take weeks off in the summer for college-trekking. We had a glorious time.

Jason drove. That assured a pleasant trip right there. He also called the coaches who had contacted him in order to arrange appointments on campuses. In the space of four days we would visit five colleges, starting with West Point.

The colonel at West Point gave Jason the insight he needed in choosing his college. This man laid it on the line:

"You have your choice open to you, Weaver. You can go to any college you choose with the grades and record and abilities you have. Choose carefully, for this decision makes the difference in the rest of your life. Make up your mind after you see them all. At the Academy you will develop leadership skills more than elsewhere. Graduates of West Point can always find a good job after their time of service. But other schools offer tremendous advantages, too. Enjoy this opportunity to see these institutions and appreciate the options you have."

Often in dealing with the grandchildren I have been most aware of how much these experiences would have thrilled John. I nearly wept at the military academy thinking how proud his grandfather would have been to hear that colonel praising Jason.

The basketball coach at Princeton, Pete Carrill, can be called the "Mr. Chips" of college sports. His interest in Jason was personal and friendly. Finally, Carrill chose to conduct the two of us on a tour of the Princeton campus.

"It's too hot to roam all over the place. I'll just show you the two most important buildings we have here, the library and the chapel."

Of course, I was ready to sign the kid up with this man right now.

Harvard and Yale held little interest on this trip, although the coach at Harvard impressed Jason very much. About Yale, he laughed. "This would be a nice place to go to school if you want to be a monk." I agreed.

Columbia in New York City took most of the next day for Jason. I watched him go off on his own to the university. Sixteen years old. New York City. Certainly he came back in one piece, but I had spent the day worrying about how he had fared in the big, dangerous city.

As soon as he came back to the hotel, his first words were, "I got to see Madison Square Garden, Oma. I stood right there in Madison Square Garden." So now you know why his presence there with the Stanford team later meant so much to both of us. The pilgrim had been to Mecca.

Almost three years later we were back in New York, he with the basketball team, me for an interview on CNN. Most convenient hotel for both of us was the Marriott on Times Square. What grandmother could have been luckier that that? Here the pilgrim had returned to Mecca, the Garden, with his team. Jason did not get to play; the games were too close for the coach to replace his starting five. Jason was only a "red-shirt freshman." But there he was in his Stanford uniform with the rest of the guys and there I sat in the stands directly behind the team. Thrilled? I'm close to tears just writing about it.

So why Stanford? Blue skies. "I couldn't stand to live back here where the skies are gray so much, Oma."

But we did have a great trip, exploring the Ivy League.

♣

II
WHERE DO WE GO FROM HERE?

Grandmothers' roles do vary. The joy is knowing we have the time and the experience at this stage of our lives to fit in in a number of ways. Some grannies are called on to take over households or at least become responsible for the day-to-day lives of their grandchildren after family crises that necessitate their total involvement. Because that has not been my lot in life, I cannot address the subject here. That's a book in itself—*Grandma Raising the Kids*. Those women who manage to provide a home life for their grandchildren have my admiration.

One of the outstanding grandmothers I know is my sister, Ann Leach. Ann has a flock of little-kid grandchildren around now. Mine are mostly grown. Two or three years ago when Ann discovered to her dismay that two of her brood were not getting along well in school in the mountain town where they live, Ann jumped right in to help. Mandy and Tod certainly did not lack the ability to learn. Ann found their schools to be lacking in motivation more than anything. She analyzed the situation; you'll have to ask her about the problems.

No matter what explanation she came up with for the deplorable state of these youngsters and their schooling, Ann knew what she could do about it. Ann has "school" on her ranch for several weeks every summer to give Tod and Mandy the incentive to learn and the skills they are missing in their own classrooms.

Of course, this pleases the children and their parents. Grammy's school is conducted on a strict schedule with regular assignments and all sorts of teaching aids. Ann is a born teacher. Everybody has a good time, but the work is real and the results have astonished the teachers at regular school when these kids return in the fall.

Projects connected with learning have impressed the entire family. Those Leach children put on a marionette show that would have knocked your eyes out. They wrote and produced this drama. The stage had been built, the marionettes made and costumed, the scripts memorized, when the entire family gathered to see the show. Wonderful. They even wrote invitations to the aunts and uncles, pleased with themselves but scarcely aware of how very much they had learned in the process. Ann has changed those lives as nobody else had the time or the capacity to do.

Speaking of grade school, I asked Jason when he was about to start kindergarten if he would miss his pre-school.

"No," he said slowly, thoughtful boy that he was, "but they'll sure miss me."

"Why, Jason?"

"They'll have to choose another biggest kid. I'm the only four-footer they've got."

Since that time, several schools have had to choose another biggest kid, but the learning process goes on.

More and more I look at our vacations together as a learning experience. As a matter of strict fact, I look at my own travels now as another learning experience, whether I am headed for Elderhostel or taking one or two grandchildren on anything from a short hike to a trip abroad. The Smithsonian provides excellent travel opportunities concentrated on learning.

For several years I drooled over the idea of a week involved in an archeological dig with two grandsons and the Smithsonian. Age limit (the lower one) was sixteen. Just as soon as Jason and Whitney turned sixteen I signed up for Crow Canyon. Whitney's mother, Allison, invited herself along, which made more fun for all of us since she and I paired off and stayed out of the way of the boys.

What a time we had. Crow Canyon lies in the Four Corners area near Mesa Verde. In residence were a staff of expert archeologists who first lectured to our group of twenty or so, then educated us to know what was pottery so we'd throw out the hard pieces of dirt, then gave each of us our own little bucket and shovel and sent us out to dig.

Each couple of students had been assigned their own plot. We didn't just run loose digging holes in the mesa. On our tablets we recorded the numbers identifying our own space, then listed whatever we found that seemed important. The process required us to fill our buckets with loose soil from our dig and strain away the dirt on a screen frame, leaving only the good stuff.

All of the crowd emptied their diggings into wheelbarrows, which became heavy later in the day. Jason and Whitney eagerly manned the wheelbarrows for the older folks, primarily in order to make more wheelbarrow time for themselves. Those sixteen-year-olds had two major accomplishments: They dug and strained more dry red dirt than anyone else in the bunch and they were allowed to drive my BMW. Even more important, they unearthed some real finds like handles from jars and large shards decorated with white and black designs from a thousand years ago, more or less.

All four of us had a great time. All four of us learned some about the people who lived in our part of the world so many years ago. We also learned why archeologists do what they do. The fascination was contagious. Housing consisted of authentic Navajo hogans for four, a large hall for lectures and dining, and one big community hogan where all the plumbing could be found.

Most of our fellow students were about as adept as we were at digging and identifying the artifacts. One fine teaching aid took place after dinner in the evenings when all sorts of treasures on long tables challenged our ability to name the early culture represented. Whit and Jason shone in that arena, too.

Often other diggers would ask opinions and advice from our boys, the only youngsters in the crowd. Allison and I just beamed when that happened until one day we overheard a young woman from Connecticut asking Whitney about small round brown objects littering the path to Duckfoot Dig.

Whit kept a straight face as he explained, "Those are rabbit berries, Irma. They come from these rabbit bushes along the side here."

These same two young men, freshmen in college, joined the Smithsonian and me for a Washington Anytime Weekend during spring break. If you find this at all possible, do it. We explored the museums and the other buildings along the Mall at leisure and had a great time. Of course they walked my legs off, but that only added to their realization that Oma isn't as young as she used to be, but that she can generally keep up, anyway.

Besides, I gathered as much new information as they did and had the rare privilege of listening to these two compare notes about their fledgling college experiences. Whitney attends Washington and Lee in Virginia, a school of the Old South to a certain extent. Jason is at Stanford.

Said Whitney, the Texan, to his cousin, "Jason, are there many minorities at your school?"

Jason thought that over. "Only me."

I'd like to spend more time with as many of my family as I can muster on a visit to the old home grounds in Kansas. Two of the grandkids, Jason and Jenny, drove with me from New York to Colorado and we stopped only briefly in McPherson and Concordia since both towns lie off the Interstate and we were "headed for the barn" by the time we had traveled halfway across Kansas. Allison and her family drove around in McPherson, but they were on the wrong streets for our family homes.

My children knew Concordia because we spent more time there. My parents had left McPherson before our children were born. As you can tell from the opening chapters of this book, McPherson's importance needs to be beefed up with the rest of my tribe. I love the memories of McPherson days, even if Sundahl's swimming pool and Hubbell's Drug Store have long since faded into local history.

Only once, so far, have I taken a grandchild abroad with me. Sarah and I went to Greece for ten days on our own—no conducted tours, no group excursions. I had been in Greece in 1984 and loved the feeling and the country in general. When Sarah chose Greece I was delighted.

Sarah was fourteen. I opted for this trip at that age—before she would want to drink or drive. We had a good time that turned out to be a learning experience in unexpected ways. Not only were we surrounded by the ruins of temples and palaces pictured on the Discovery Channel or PBS; we found ourselves among people of most European nationalities, but no Americans.

Only shopkeepers and taxi drivers and a few hotel clerks spoke any English at all. For a fourteen-year-old an ocean away from her phone and her friends, truly this was a learning experience in being in the minority. We were also so much in the minority on the beaches among females of all ages wearing only the bottoms of their swim suits that we finally gave up on the beaches. Mutual unspoken consent.

We did, however, absorb much of the culture in Athens, Crete, and Rhodes before we had to head home for cheerleading camp. Instead of hooking up with any tour company, I called the travel service of American Express to arrange our trip.

I cannot say enough good about those people. One girl in their office handled arrangements from start to finish as soon as I told her where we wanted to go, what sort of hotels we preferred (not the fanciest!), and our available time. Even airport transfers and luggage handling were provided in each place. Our hotels met our needs perfectly, especially since two meals were included with rooms. Local Amex offices obligingly cared for any other requests we had. I am certain we saved money with this service and we certainly saved ourselves time and trouble.

Greek food did not turn Sarah on, I must say. She picked at most of it, which was to be expected even though we had tried a Greek restaurant in New York just to get some idea of what we were facing. Greece has no McDonald's, which I considered to be an advantage until Sarah found eating most Greek food distasteful.

Of course, there were French fries and a few other staples of the teen-age diet. The evening Sarah and I strolled down past the white stucco buildings with red roofs and festoons of bouganvillaea into the special seafood buffet in the seaside taverna of the hotel on Crete—picture moonlight on the bay, oleanders and hibiscus in bloom, excellent Greek music live in our midst—all this seemed promising until we both spotted raw octopus draped on the canopy over the barbecue. They resembled bats with suction cups. No American teen could have endured such a sight. Sarah did enjoy taking part in the Greek dancing, but dinner was a complete bust.

I intend to wait until a year after our Greek vacation to question Sarah about the lasting effects of such travel. Over-all, I'd say we accomplished a lot. Most important, we learned much more about each other and shared more conversation about more subjects in those few days than we had in the last ten years. That counts.

Traveling with the grand-family has taken on much more importance in the past few years. Two reasons. Retired grandparents have longer life expectancy and more leisure time than earlier generations. (We also stay healthier longer.) Few parents can spend that much time, let alone money, in families where both parents work. New set of facts of life for many of us, isn't it?

Planning group travel experiences for grandparents and their grandchildren has become a business on its own. Agencies like Grandtravel in Bethesda, Maryland, concentrate on such family-oriented vacations-with-learning. I just might try that next. At least, the kid will have somebody besides me to talk to.

Quite aside from travel experiences with their children, I must stick in a word here about the good times I have with my daughters-in-law when we have shared being on the road together. Often overlooked might be the chance to get to know your son's wife as a real person, not simply a cog in the family machinery, if you get lucky enough to drive long distances together or share time away from both of your homes. I never realized what delightful women my sons had married until I had enough time without the children or the husbands or the daily routines of either of us to allow us to become truly acquainted. Now we are good friends.

Such might not be possible with a son-in-law. My own experience with Allison's husband has been more than cordial, but I doubt he'd want to drive cross-country or even raft down a river with Oma. Besides, that's more family life than this one book can cover.

❧

12
WHEN I GROW TOO OLD TO DREAM

W*hen I grow too old to dream, I'll have you to remember* . . . Grandmother Allison's favorite song, that Rudolph Friml hit. She used to ask Mary Marn to sing it, often. Now I hear it in my head. Driving along a highway, hurrying through a shower, facing a friendly audience, lying alone in the dark, I hear those words and that tune.

Particularly, I have been aware of the lyrics while writing this book. Facing the years past, looking at the fine time I'm having as a grandmother, but more especially facing the future, there's a basic truth there: When I grow too old to dream, I'll have you to remember.

Right now I am sixty-seven. That's not old enough to attract attention or to cause comment. Lifespans have stretched 'way beyond these years of mine. Perhaps mine will, too. But I do feel old enough, experienced enough at living, that building memories is a great part of what life is about now. Not just my own memories of family, friends, books, speeches and mini-TV series. I'm talking lasting memories in the lives of the people I've touched.

Shared memories are the basis for all of my carrying-on with these grandkids. When I have been with Sarah in Greece or with Jenny and Jason at Niagara Falls, most of all that has been learning, sharing, which we alone have in the midst of the family. I have no doubt there will be times after I've died when the younger family members will recall unpleasant or difficult times with me. I'm not trying to be Mary Poppins or Ma Perkins. Not even Tinker Bell.

More than any other recollection, I hope to be thought of as one person who added something positive to their lives.

This has a lot to do with love, but very little to do with obligation. Years ago I heard an old lady say, "write anything you want on my tombstone, just please don't say, 'She meant well.'"

Like the song I just mentioned, that rings in my head a lot. None of the fun, the pleasure I have enjoyed with my family, has come from a sense of "I ought to do something nice for these people because we're related." Instead, the trips, the games, have been as much for my own amusement as for theirs. I just hoped to choose the right venture for mixed generations. After all, I'll be too old to dream long before they reach that stage.

Back in grade school we had some sort of a game where the code words were "pass it on." Remember that? It occurs to me those are the code words for grandmothers. Pass it on. All of the good I recall from my own grandmother I have tried to pass along to my grandchildren. Certainly I cannot claim 100 per cent success. My grandmother career resembles the rest of my life: some of it on target and a lot of near misses. Still, I trust these generations will pass it on.

I can picture Ross and Judy climbing around Mesa Verde with Sarah's sons, or Chris and Mary showing the wonders of the Grand Canyon to a grandchild some day. Or perhaps just making cookies with a messy, happy little girl will be Allison's joy in grandparenting.

Who knows?

Just pass it on.

♣

Keep reading!
An excerpt from
Frances Weaver's
next book follows!

GOLDEN ROAMERS
The Unpublished Journal
of Lillian Morrison

*You'll enjoy Frances's first novel—about how residents of a
landlocked, ocean-motif retirement village cruise the
country in a bus they, well, borrowed!*

GOLDEN ROAMERS
will be published early in 1992.
Order your copy now from your favorite bookseller
or from

MIDLIFE MUSINGS

P.O. Box 970
Saratoga Springs, New York 12866
(800) 842-7229

We pick up the story shortly after chapter 1 begins . . .

So here we go. Bess, Ruth and I headed for Redlands, and you are welcome to come along for the ride.

First of all, we saw George Schroeder walking along Hornblower Boulevard on his way to the bus stop. He always looks happier on Tuesdays and Fridays because those are his holidays. Busman's holidays. George rides the bus twice a week. Sometimes in one direction. Sometimes another. But George loves those "coaches." We've spotted him sometimes, always sitting right behind the driver, talking a blue streak. Probably about his stops in Pennsylvania: Annville, Lebanon, Hershey. We know that routine by heart.

Like every Tuesday, Bess pulled up beside George and stuck her head out the window.

"Can we give you a lift, George? We're headed for Redlands this morning."

Just like always, George grinned and shook his head.

"No. Thank you kindly, Miss Ferguson. I'll leave the driving to Trailways today. Going over to Riverside. Nice park there, and the old Mission Inn."

George could be the archetypical Pennsylvania Dutchman. Round face, sober demeanor. I half expect him to say something like "it wonders me if it will make down rain" or to order shoo-fly pie at the Captain's Mess. If they had shoo-fly pie it wouldn't be as fine as Esther's. We can be sure of that. George gave us his bus (coach) operator's wave and we were off.

The drive to Redlands takes just under an hour. Close to fifty miles, which makes it perfect for us. Plenty of time to catch up on our visiting but not long enough to get bored with the ride. Sitting right here at my desk at this unaccustomed hour, scribbling on this journal as fast as I can go, I know I'll never be bored on that road again. Not after today.

"Just get to the point, Lil!" My husband used to yell that at me all the time. But I think details make a better story. However, we can skip over the hairdresser part except that in the parking lot we all got the giggles watching a darling little nun riding a three-wheeled bike with a big basket on it. Ruth said she'd seen her before, but Bess and I stared. Not any bigger than a minute, but she could get that clumsy bike up and down the hills around there like a teenager. I never can guess the ages of nuns, particularly the few left who wear the full habit. But this tiny person had to be in her 70s, at least.

We did a little shopping, no buying. Then we went to our favorite deli and sat out for a really great lunch. Bess sat there gazing into space.

"You know," Bess said, "Not far from here I bet I could show you girls an old mansion where my cousins and sisters and I used to play. Nobody lived there. We could roam around and peek in the windows and pretend we were movie stars who owned such a grand place. On Sunset Drive, maybe. I'd almost forgotten about that. Instead of driving out around the university and all that, how about exploring?"

That suited me fine, of course. I didn't have a husband to worry about any longer, but Ruth had a kind of skeptical look.

"If it doesn't make us late," she said. "You know how Emmett gets if we are not back by three."

Did we *ever* know how "Emmett gets"! Just once last May was enough for Bess and me.

❧

Bess paid for lunch from our Girls' Day Out kitty. We had decided from the very first of these outings we'd have a Tuesday fund, which we all shared. Kind of funny how it started. After our first lunch together, each one of us reached for our purses. Then we heard a bunch of old ladies at the next table splitting their bill. One old gal had a high, squawky voice. She bellered something about "Georgene had the crab salad." Didn't take the three of us long to work out our finances better than that.

Driving through the old, rich-folks' part of Redlands was a joy. Bess kept saying, "Now, I remember . . ."

Just as we headed up Sunset, however, we all yelled at once. There beside the road knelt our little nun. The chain had slipped off her bike and she was struggling to get it back in place.

Bess stopped immediately, of course, and we all jumped out. In less time than it takes to tell it, my two friends were down on the ground beside Sister Anne. (Later she told us her name, but we felt then as if we knew her.)

You never saw such a smile. She absolutely beamed when she realized we wanted to help. I just stood there. What do I know about chains on bicycles? I did think I might direct traffic if another car came along.

Bess and Ruth were having the time of their lives.

Ruth introduced the three of us and said, "We noticed you and your bike at the shopping center earlier, Sister. You ride extremely well." You could tell she stopped just short of saying, ". . . for a woman your age." Sister Anne could tell that, too. She nodded at all of us.

"I ride down every morning to the post office to collect the mail for the convent and to run a few errands as I need to. This chain slips every once in a while. It's not far up to the convent from here and I often have to walk the bike back up where Mike can fix it for me. How nice for me this afternoon that you ladies came along. The walk all the way up can be wearing in the heat of the day."

Bess had the chain on where it belonged. She wiped her hands on her blue denim skirt and gave the tiny nun a big grin.

"Sister, I'd like to test drive this chain to make sure it's okay now. We don't want you having any spills. I haven't ridden a bike like this in years, but what do you say you ride on up the hill with my two friends in the car and I'll follow on your velocipede, here? Okay? Ruth, the keys are in the ignition."

That holy sister fairly radiated when Bess suggested that.

The drive on up Sunset wound past eucalyptus trees and tangled old oleanders. Some spacious, fancy houses lined the avenue until we got near the top where a long stucco wall in need of many repairs cut off the view of grounds inside. Right ahead of us I could see a huge pink mansion-type structure. I leaned up to tap Ruth on the shoulder. "Do you suppose that's the mansion Bess used to play around? Looks pretty deserted to me."

Sister Anne was so short I couldn't even see her from the back seat. "Straight ahead?" Now I could see her bony finger, pointing.

"That, ladies, is our convent. Our order is St. Ives. Of course, this is not the Mother House. That's in upstate New York. Mr Burrage built this house here in Redlands many years ago—a real showplace, I'd say. He left the property to the church. Bless him, but the upkeep has been almost too much for the sisterhood these past years."

You can say that again, I thought. The whole place had turned into a jungle. We drove up the drive past the biggest barn this side of Santa Anita, and I figured it would take a machete and six bulldozers to clear a path to where the tennis courts must have been. No wonder old Burrage left it to the church. His kids surely didn't want it, and in the depression nobody would buy a white elephant like this.

That was mean of me to think that way. Still, I could see what must have been so wonderful to Bess when she was a kid.

Speaking of Bess, she was all tuckered out, as they might say back in

Kansas City, when she reached the top of that hill. "Little lady, you are some cyclist," she gasped at Sister Anne.

Ruth picked up the sacks in the basket behind the seat. "Nothing in here but cat food," she whispered to me. "Do you have the mail in this sack, Sister?" she said aloud.

Sister Anne forced her magic smile. "There wasn't any."

At the sound of Sister's voice, cats appeared as if on cue. Cats came from everywhere. The barn, the weeds, the porches, the terrace overlooking Redlands and the valley—all alive with cats. Any color, any size, any stage of pregnancy.

Sister Anne bent to touch each one as cats surrounded her in the drive. "Order of St. Ives," she said with a smile.

Well, Ruth kept checking her watch so Bess and I knew we had to cut this short. We refused the offer of a conducted tour of the decrepit mansion but promised to return the next Tuesday, earlier in the day. "Why don't you wait for us next Tuesday, Sister? That way you can ride with us and give your bike a rest." Bess really has a way with words, doesn't she?

Hell-bent for Snug Harbor, we hoped to be no more than fifteen minutes late at the most. Emmett would be standing out by their mailbox. Damn.

Note: I am 69. Have I told you that? In my first 69 years I have learned just two really good lessons.

The first: Don't sweat the small stuff.

The second: Don't expect the rest of the world to do what you know you have to do for yourself.

Simple? It works for me so far, even if it took me most of three score and ten to figure that much out. So here I am, 69 years old, still up 'way past my usual bedtime scribbling away here so I won't forget the details of this extraordinary day.

You might have thought the meeting-the-nun story made Tuesday a big day, but that was only the first half. Believe me, it gets even better.

❧

About halfway home to Snug Harbor, between Beaumont and Banning, we were zipping along I-10. Bess was really pushing, trying to get Ruth home before Emmett exploded. All of a sudden she slammed on the brakes and almost swerved off the road. Ruth and I had been chatting, trying not to put any more pressure on Bess. Generally speaking, Bess is a careful driver. We all are. Not that we are protecting our lives so much; we just want these cars to last. So this maneuver of Bess's brought us to attention in a hurry. I almost said, "What the hell?" but Ruth beat me to it. I realized I was shaking.

"Over there! Look back! No, on the other side of the road—the other lane! See him? George! George Schroeder! Our friend George!"

Bess was certainly worked up. I had never seen her so excited before.

She had slowed now to make an illegal U-turn to get into the eastbound lane back toward Beaumont.

"See him, Ruth?" She had scared the daylights out of two Toyotas and a Chevy pickup by careening across three lanes of traffic in front of them to get to the far right lane.

"You mean that man standing beside that big bus?"

"Are you sure that's Schroeder?" I asked, because Ruth and I were not sure of anything. Bess might have flipped out at the prospect of facing Emmett being mad at us again.

I tried to be the calm one. "Now, what would a meek and mild little man like George Schroeder be doing standing out on a superhighway in all of this traffic, waving his arms like a madman and pointing to a hellishly big bus? Bess, are you sure—?"

Bess didn't have to answer. By that time she had pulled up behind the bus and jumped out of her car. Thank heaven she ran to the right side of the bus away from the roaring, speeding traffic. (*Is that starboard? I remember thinking.*) Sure enough, here came George, looking as if he had spent all day in a demolition derby. He was beat.

"Oh, I just prayed you ladies would come along. Thank you. Thank you for stopping. I need your help. I do need your help." Ruth looked like she might faint. One more delay, and Emmett—

"Now, George, just calm down here a bit and get your breath." Bess patted his arm. "The girls and I are on our way home but we'll do what we can. First, in one short sentence, what's the problem?"

George took a deep breath, which almost did him in. "That coach." He pointed as if we might not have noticed he was jumping like a puppet next to one gigantic "cruiser."

"That coach broke down this morning. The driver was a young twerp who had no appreciation for such a fine piece of—"

"Easy here, George. Just the pertinent facts. So the bus won't go. Now what on earth does that have to do with us? I figured you need a ride home. That's why I stopped. Is there more to the story?" Bess Ferguson must have been a fine teacher. No wonder her girls won the tournaments.

"Sure, there's more to the story!" I guess you could say George just blurted that out. "The dumb-bunny rookie operator left me to guard this coach while he went off to call the dispatcher for help. That was almost six hours ago. The other passengers—I'll tell you about that later—now it's been six hours and not one soul has showed up. I don't think he even called. Probably scared they'd fire him, so he quit and walked away. That's my guess. These youngsters have no idea of the value of—"

"George!" I had to interrupt. We had to get home.

"Okay. I must protect this coach until it can be returned to the company barns. It's only a vapor lock. This baby will run fine now. All I need to do is move her out of harm's way. If we let her stay here all night she'll be vandalized by morning—tires slashed, windows shattered. These Californians are crazy."

Well, he's just a short little Pennsylvania Dutchman, and a lonely one at that, but as George got that gleam in his eye I knew no bus ever had a more dedicated protector than this one right here.

Ruth had long since stopped worrying about what Emmett might say. She already knew, anyway. "George," she said carefully, "You have spent the entire day contemplating this bus and this predicament. What do you suggest? What is the next move?"

"Ah, Ruth. Good question." Never before had he called her by her first name. Or any name, for that matter. "See that shed, that packing barn, over there? Just off the access? Looks to me as if that place is empty and will just about fit this vehicle. If we could arrange to leave her there for the night I could drive her over myself. Then tomorrow morning we could decide how best to—"

"Great." Bess had had enough conversation. "I'll go talk to the man I see out in front there, and then signal you to drive on over. I suppose you've driven lots of busses this size, haven't you, George?"

"Oh, no, Miss Ferguson. All my life I dreamed of driving the Interstate. Now thinking of driving this beauty just around the corner to that—Esther would be so proud."

"Just don't cry, George," I whispered to Ruth. "I don't think I can take watching a grown man cry over a vapor-locked bus."

❧

We were back in the car and Bess was rehearsing her speech to the owner of the barn. At the same time I had a feeling Bess was tumbling a lot of other thoughts about busses around in her brain. Made me think of the rock tumbler John bought for the kids and set it up in our garage. For months on end that contraption sat there tumbling rocks and nobody ever opened it to peek in to see what had happened to the rocks. Just gazing at the back of Bess's head, I could tell her tumbler was about to come up with some sort of a polished gem of an idea. Somehow that gave me the shivers.

Bess and Ruth worked the deal about the barn. I stayed in the car, thinking about whatever could be done with a 46-passenger bus that might fall into one's possession like manna from heaven.

My two companions were so animated in their negotiations with the brusk, dirty barnkeeper, I could almost guess what they were thinking, too.

Abruptly, Bess pulled out our Girls' Day Out purse and gave the man all the money we had left. Hey, I almost yelled, that's our lunch money for the next six weeks! But Ruth and Bess were both waving wildly at George over on the highway, so I kept quiet.

We all watched almost reverently as George Schroeder wheeled that enormous baby into that narrow garage with inches to spare on either side. "You're so right, George. Esther would be most proud," I said to nobody in particular.

❧

Now it's really late. I'll have to tell you in the morning about the conversation on the ride home and Emmett's tantrum later. This probably won't make sense when I read it over tomorrow, but at least I've got most of the day on paper.

Quite a day for a bunch of old fogies washed ashore at Snug Harbor.

🐚